Choose the Perfect

For my patient, supportive and grounded husband Adam, who certainly lives up to the meaning of his name: earth.

Choose the Perfect Baby Name

Victoria Wilson

Hodder Education
338 Euston Road, London NW1 3BH.

Hodder Education is an Hachette UK company

First published in UK 2008 by Hodder Education

First published in US 2008 by The McGraw-Hill Companies, Inc.

This edition published 2011.

British Library Cataloguing in Publication Data: a catalogue record for this
title is available from the British Library.

Library of Congress Catalog Card Number: on file.

10 9 8 7 6 5 4 3 2

The publisher has used its best endeavours to ensure that any website
addresses referred to in this book are correct and active at the time of going
to press. However, the publisher and the author have no responsibility for
the websites and can make no guarantee that a site will remain live or that
the content will remain relevant, decent or appropriate.

The publisher has made every effort to mark as such all words which it
believes to be trademarks. The publisher should also like to make it clear
that the presence of a word in the book, whether marked or unmarked,
in no way affects its legal status as a trademark.

Every reasonable effort has been made by the publisher to trace the copyright
holders of material in this book. Any errors or omissions should be notified
in writing to the publisher, who will endeavour to rectify the situation for
any reprints and future editions.

Hachette UK's policy is to use papers that are natural, renewable and
recyclable products and made from wood grown in sustainable forests.
The logging and manufacturing processes are expected to conform to the
environmental regulations of the country of origin.

www.hoddereducation.co.uk

Typeset by MPS Limited, a Macmillan Company.

Printed in Great Britain by CPI Antony Rowe, Chippenham and Eastbourne.

Front cover: © Judith Thomandl/imagebroker/Alamy

Back cover: © Jakub Semeniuk/iStockphoto.com, © Royalty-Free/
Corbis, © agencyby/iStockphoto.com, © Andy Cook/iStockphoto.com,
© Christopher Ewing/iStockphoto.com, © zebicho – Fotolia.com,
© Geoffrey Holman/iStockphoto.com, © Photodisc/Getty Images,
© James C. Pruitt/iStockphoto.com, © Mohamed Saber – Fotolia.com

Contents

Meet the author

When I began writing this book of baby names, my daughter Carys (Welsh, a nod to my Celtic connections) was two and my youngest son, Jem (name inspired by a literary character), was just a few months old. I was therefore very aware of just how daunting and exciting this task of finding a name for your baby can be. For parents like myself, who have long daydreamed about the possibilities of names for daughters and sons, it was a thoroughly enjoyable task at first.

But as I trawled through the available lists of names, I soon became aware of two problems. Firstly, I couldn't find many resources where names were divided into smaller categories, but also available in one long alphabetical list. I thought a list like this would allow me to browse in different ways according to the different ideas and moods I went through before I finally settled on my decision. Secondly, I found that the meanings of names varied hugely. Many lists and books seemed to conjure the original meanings from the air.

I've therefore organized this book in a way that is helpful and inspiring whether you are looking for a name that gives a nod towards your cultural roots, one that won't date as your child grows up, or if you just want a name that begins with a C. I've also cross-referenced each and every name in the book to try to find its most popular meaning. In doing this, I've discovered that even the experts disagree on the meanings of names. This is because some name meanings are open to different interpretation, and because many names have changed so much over the centuries that they bear little resemblance to the word they were originally taken from. Take the name Mary for example. Linguistically, the name comes from the Latin for bitter. Some people have therefore stated that it means 'bitterly wanted child', but this is not what the name actually means, it's just someone's interpretation of it. Another example of how meanings change over time can be seen in the name Rebecca, which means heifer in Hebrew. The cultural meaning of a cow to the ancient Hebrew population is very different from the connotations of calling a girl a cow today!

I hope you find the name you're looking for in the pages of this book and, whatever your decision, know that the name you choose will never be the wrong one, because within just a few hours of giving it to your baby, it will be a word that means everything to you.

1

Boys' names
A to Z

A

Name	Alternative spellings	Origin	Meaning
Aaron		Hebrew	Exalted one
Abbas	Ab, Abba	Arabic	Harsh
Abbondanzio		Italian	Plentiful
Abbondio		Italian	Plentiful
Abbott	Abbitt, Abott	Hebrew	Father
Abdalla		African	Servant of God
Abdel	Abdiel	Arabic	Servant
Abdul	Ab, Abul	African	Servant of the Lord
Abdullah	Abdallah	Arabic	The servant of Allah
Abe	Abey	Hebrew	From Abraham, father of many
Abedi		African	Worshipper
Abejundio		Spanish	Like a bee
Abel	Abe	Hebrew	Breath, vapour. Murdered by his brother, Cain, in the Bible
Abelard	Abe, Abellard	German	Firm

Name	Alternative spellings	Origin	Meaning
Abelardo		Italian	Like a bee
Abele		Italian	White poplar
Aberdeen		Place name	Scottish city
Aberforth		Scottish	Mouth of the River Forth
Abiola		African	Born in honour
Abir		Arabic	The fragrant one
Abner	Abnor	Hebrew	Father of light
Abraham	Abe	Hebrew	Father of a multitude
Abram	Abrahm, Abe	Hebrew	Father of a multitude
Abramo		Italian	Father of a multitude
Ace		American	Nickname for someone who's the best
Achilles		Greek	Legendary warrior in Greek mythology
Acorn		English	The seed of an oak tree
Adalfredo		Italian	He who protects his descendants
Adalgiso		Italian	Precious promise
Adalrico		Italian	Noble ruler
Adam	Addam	Hebrew	Red earth
Addison		Hebrew	Son of Adam
Adelbert		German	Noble and bright
Adil		Arabic	Just, fair
Adnan		Arabic	The settler
Adolf	Adolph	German	Noble wolf
Adoni		Australian	Sunset
Adonis		Greek	Beautiful man. Lover of Venus
Adrian	Ade, Adrien	Latin	Dark, rich, from Hadria in Italy
Adriano		Italian	Dark, rich, from Hadria in Italy

Name	Alternative spellings	Origin	Meaning
Adriel	Adrial, Adryal	Hebrew	God's follower
Afanasi		Russian	Immortal
Afram		African	A river in Ghana
Agatino		Italian	Good
Agustin		Spanish	Great, magnificent
Ahmed		Arabic	Most highly praised
Ahron		Hebrew	Exalted one
Aidan	Adan	Irish	Fiery one
Aimé		French	Loved
Ainsley		Anglo-Saxon	My own meadow
Ajax		Greek	Mythical Greek hero
Akama		Australian	A whale
Akbar		Arabic	Great
Ake		Scandinavian	Ancestor
Akeem		Arabic	Ruler
Akil		Arabic	Intelligent
Akim		Russian	Joachim
Akram		Arabic	Generous, noble
Al		From several names, Alan, Alfred, etc.	
Aladdin		Arabic	A servant of Allah
Alain		French	Handsome
Alan		Scottish, Irish	Handsome
Alarico		Italian, Spanish	Rules all
Alasdair	Alastair	Scottish	Defender of mankind
Alban		Latin	White
Alberico		Italian	Noble and bright
Albert		Anglo-Saxon	Noble and bright
Alberto		Italian	Noble and bright
Albion		Latin	White, poetic name for Britain
Albus		Latin	White

Name	Alternative spellings	Origin	Meaning
Alden		Anglo-Saxon	Old friend
Aldo		Italian	Old
Aldon		Anglo-Saxon	Old friend
Aldous		German	Old
Aldwin		Anglo-Saxon	Old friend
Alec		French	Defender of mankind
Alejandro		Spanish	Defender of mankind
Alek		Russian	Defender of mankind
Aleksander		Russian	Defender of mankind
Aleksei		Russian	Defender of mankind
Aleppo		Place name	City in Syria
Aleron		French	Knight
Alessio		Italian	Defender of mankind
Alex		Greek	Defender of mankind
Alexander		Greek	Defender of mankind
Alexandre		French	Defender of mankind
Alexei		Russian	Defender of mankind
Alexis		Greek	Defender of mankind
Alfie		Anglo-Saxon	From Alfred, elf. wise counsellor
Alfonso		Italian, Spanish	Ready for battle
Alfred		Anglo-Saxon	Elf, wise counsellor
Alfredo		Italian	Wise counsellor
Algar		Anglo-Saxon	Elf spear
Alger		Anglo-Saxon	Elf spear
Ali		Arabic	Exalted
Alim		Arabic	Wise
Alistair		Scottish	Defender of mankind
Alister		Irish	Defender of mankind
Allambee		Australian	A quiet resting place
Allan	Allyn, Alan, Alun, Allen	Irish	Handsome
Alonso		Spanish	Noble and ready
Alun	Allyn, Alan, Allen	Welsh	Handsome

4

Name	Alternative spellings	Origin	Meaning
Alvaro		Italian, Spanish	Speaker of truth
Alvin		Anglo-Saxon	Elf friend
Alwyn		Anglo-Saxon	Elf friend
Amadeus		Latin	Loves God. Name of Wolfgang Amadeus Mozart, famous composer
Amador		Spanish	Lover
Amal		Arabic	Hope
Amalio		Italian	Lively, determined
Amaranto		Italian	Long lived
Amaroo		Australian	A beautiful place
Amato		Spanish	Beloved
Amaury		French	Hard-working, powerful
Ambar		Sanskrit	Of the sky
Ambrose		Greek	Immortal
America		Place name	America is named after Italian explorer Amerigo Vespucci
Amerigo		Italian	Home ruler
Amin		Arabic	Honest and trustworthy
Amir		Arabic	Prince
Amis		French	Variant of Ames, friend
Amistad		Spanish	Friendship
Amory		German	Ruler of the home
Amos		Hebrew	Borne by God
Amrit		Sanskrit	The immortal one
Amund		Scandinavian	Feared protector
Anand		Sanskrit	Joyful
Anatole		Greek	From the East
Ancel		French	Servant
Anders		Scandinavian	Manly

Name	Alternative spellings	Origin	Meaning
André		French	Manly
Andrei		Russian	Manly
Andrew	Andy, Drew	Greek	Manly
Andy		Greek	Manly
Angelo		Italian	Angel
Anghus	Angus	Scottish	Exceptionally strong
Anil		Sanskrit	Of the wind
Anisim		Russian	Beneficial, profitable
Ansari		Arabic	A helper
Anselm		German	God's helmet
Anthony	Tony	Latin	Worthy of praise
Antoine		French	Praiseworthy
Anton		French	Praiseworthy
Antonio		Italian, Spanish	Worthy of praise
Anwar		Arabic	The bright one
Anwell		Welsh	Beloved
Anwyl		Welsh	Beloved
Aonghus		Celtic	Exceptionally strong
Apollo		Greek	God of poetry, music and healing
Aragorn		Literary	*The Lord of the Rings* by J. R. R. Tolkien
Araluen		Australian	The place of water lilies
Aram		Hebrew	Father of a multitude
Aramis		Literary	*The Three Musketeers* by Alexandre Dumas
Arcadio		Greek	Man from Arcadia, paradise
Archibald	Archie, Baldie	German	Genuine, brave
Archie		Scottish	Genuine, brave
Archimedes		Greek	To think about first
Arcturus		Greek	Bear driver. The star which follows the Great Bear constellation

Name	Alternative spellings	Origin	Meaning
Ardent		English	Keen
Argus		Greek	In mythology, a giant with 100 eyes
Ari	Are	Scandinavian	Eagle
Ariel		Hebrew	Lion of God
Aries		Greek	The ram. A star sign and constellation
Ariki		Pacific Islands	Chief
Arion	Ari Arie	Greek	Enchanted man
Ariosto		Italian	Quick to fight
Aristo		Greek	Best
Arizona		Place name	US state
Arjun		Sanskrit	The white one
Arlin	Arlyn	Welsh	Vow
Armand	Armande	French	From the army
Armando		Italian, Spanish	Of the army
Armani		French	Warrior. Surname of fashion designer, Giorgio Armani
Armstrong		Anglo-Saxon	Strong-armed
Arnaud		French	Eagle power
Arnold	Arnie	German	Eagle, ruler
Aron		Hebrew	Exalted one
Arran		Place name	From the Isle of Arran
Artemas	Artie	Greek	From Artemis, goddess of the moon and hunting
Arthur	Artur	Welsh, Cornish	Bear
Artie		Welsh, Cornish	Bear
Arun		Sanskrit	The dawn
Arvid		Scandinavian	Eagle, tree
Ash		Anglo-Saxon	A tree
Ashley	Ash	Anglo-Saxon	From the meadow of ash trees

Name	Alternative spellings	Origin	Meaning
Ashok		Sanskrit	Without sadness
Ashraf		Arabic	Honourable
Asim		Arabic	The protector
Asmund		Scandinavian	Divine protection
Aston		Anglo-Saxon	Eastern town
Aswad		Arabic	Black
Athan		Greek	Immortal
Atiu		Pacific Islands	Firstborn
Aubrey	Aubry, Aubree	Anglo-Saxon	Elfin king
Auden		Anglo-Saxon	Old friend
Audey		American	Famous US soldier
Auguste		French	Noble, magnificent
Augustin		French	Noble, magnificent
Aurelius		Latin	The golden one
Austell		Place name	Cornish town, St Austell
Austin	Austen, Ostin, Ostyn	Latin	From Augustine, great, magnificent
Avalon		Celtic	An island paradise in Celtic mythology
Avery		Anglo-Saxon	Elfin king
Avon		Place name	From several English rivers
Axel		Scandinavian	Father of peace
Azim		Arabic	Grand
Aziz		Arabic	The powerful one
Azriel		Hebrew	God helps

B

Name	Alternative spellings	Origin	Meaning
Baakir		African	Eldest
Babu		African	Grandfather
Babylon		Place name	Ancient city in the Middle East
Badrani		African	Full Moon
Bailey		French	Bailiff
Bairrie		Irish	Fair-haired or marksman
Balthasar	Balthazar	Greek	The Lord protects the king. One of the three wise men
Balun		Australian	A river
Banjora		Australian	A koala
Barclay		Anglo-Saxon	From the birch tree meadow
Bardan	Barden	Welsh	Singer, poet
Bardo		Australian	Water
Barega		Australian	The wind
Barlow		American	Lives on a bare hill
Barnabas	Barney, Barny	Greek	Son of consolation
Barnaby	Barney, Barny	Greek	Son of consolation
Barney	Barnie	Anglo-Saxon	Son of comfort
Baron		Anglo-Saxon	Young warrior
Barrington		Place name	Name of English villages
Barry	Barrie	Irish	Fair head, marksman
Bartemius	Bartie	Anglo-Saxon	Hill, furrow
Bartholomew	Bart, Bartie	Anglo-Saxon	Ploughman
Barton		Anglo-Saxon	From the barley town
Barwon		Australian	Wide river
Bashir		Arabic	A good omen
Basil		Greek	Like a king

Name	Alternative spellings	Origin	Meaning
Basim		Arabic	The smiling one
Basso		Italian	Low
Baxter		Anglo-Saxon	Baker
Beau		French	Handsome
Beaumont		French	From the beautiful mountain
Beethoven		Anglo-Saxon	Famous composer
Bello		African	Helper
Ben		Latin	Son
Benedict		Latin	Blessed
Benesek		Cornish	Blessed
Benito		Italian	Blessed
Benjamin	Ben	Latin	Born of the right hand
Bennet		Latin	Blessed
Bennett		Latin	Blessed
Benno		Italian	Blessed
Benoît		French	Blessed
Benson	Ben	Latin	Blessed
Benton		Anglo-Saxon	Town in the bent grass
Bernard		Anglo-Saxon	Brave as a bear
Bernardo		Italian	Brave as a bear
Bernhard	Bernie	German	Strong as a bear
Berthold	Bert	German	Bright, splendid
Bertoldo		Italian	Illustrious leader
Bertram		Anglo-Saxon	Bright raven
Bertrand		French	Bright raven
Bevan	Bevin, Bevyn	Welsh	Young warrior
Bharat		Sanskrit	The Hindu God of fire
Bhima		Sanskrit	The mighty one
Biagio		Italian	One who stammers
Bilal		Arabic	Follower of Mohammed
Bill		Anglo-Saxon	Strong protector
Billy	Billie	Anglo-Saxon	Strong protector

Name	Alternative spellings	Origin	Meaning
Bjorn		Scandinavian	Bear
Blaine	Blane, Blayne	Irish	Slender
Blair	Blare, Blaire	Irish	Lives on the plain
Blaise	Blaze, Blaisey, Blazey	Latin	One who stammers
Blake		Anglo-Saxon	Black
Blanket		Celebrity child	(Michael Jackson)
Blayney	Blaney, Blainey	Irish	Slender
Blue		English	Primary colour
Bobby	Bob	Anglo-Saxon	From Robert, bright fame
Boden		Welsh	Blonde
Bogdan		Russian	Gift from God
Bond		Anglo-Saxon	Peasant farmer
Bones		American	Means 'bones', as in the English
Bonifacio		Italian	Good destiny
Booker		American	Bookmaker
Boone		American	Wild-west frontier hero
Boris		Russian	Famous warrior
Bosley		Anglo-Saxon	From the grove
Boston		Place name	American city
Bowden		Welsh	Blonde
Bowen	Bowyn	Welsh	Son of Owen
Bowie		Welsh	Yellow haired
Boyd		Scottish	Fair haired
Brad		American	Clearing in the wood
Bradan		Welsh	Raven
Bradford		Anglo-Saxon	Broad ford
Bradley		American	Broad forest clearing
Bram		Welsh	Raven
Bramwell		Anglo-Saxon	Broom well
Bran	Brann	Welsh	Raven
Brando		American	Talented

Name	Alternative spellings	Origin	Meaning
Brandon		Anglo-Saxon	Gorse hill
Branson		Anglo-Saxon	Son of Brandon
Brant		American	From Brent, hilltop
Brave		English	Courageous
Brecon		Place name	From Brecon Beacons in Wales
Brendan		Irish	Raven
Brennan		Welsh	Little raven
Brent		Welsh	Hilltop
Bret	Brett	Welsh	From Brittany
Brian	Bryan	Irish, Scottish	High, noble
Brighton		Place name	Seaside town on south coast of England
Brock		Anglo-Saxon	Badger
Broder	Brody	Scandinavian	Brother
Broderick		Irish	Son of a famous ruler
Brody		Irish	A ditch
Bron		Anglo-Saxon	Brown or dark
Bronson		Anglo-Saxon	Son of the dark man
Bronze		Anglo-Saxon	Precious metal
Brook		Anglo-Saxon	A small stream
Brooklyn		Place name	Area in New York. Also celebrity child (David and Victoria Beckham)
Brown		Anglo-Saxon	Colour
Bruno		German, Italian	Brown
Bryan	Brian	Irish, Scottish	High, noble
Bryce		Welsh	Strength
Bryn		Welsh	Hill
Bubba		American	Slang for baby
Buck		American	Slang for a dollar
Bud		Anglo-Saxon	Brother
Buddy		Anglo-Saxon	Brother
Butch		American	Macho
Byron		Anglo-Saxon	At the cowshed

C

Name	Alternative spellings	Origin	Meaning
Cadan		Welsh	Warrior
Cade		Literary	*Gone with the Wind* by Margaret Mitchell
Cador		Cornish	Warrior
Cadwur		Welsh	Warrior
Caelum		Latin	Constellation named after a sculptor's chisel
Cai		Welsh	Joy
Cain	Cane	Hebrew	Gatherer. Son of Adam and Eve who killed his brother in the Bible
Caio		Welsh	Joy
Cairo		Place name	Capital of Egypt
Cal		Scottish, Irish	Dove
Cale		Hebrew	From Caleb, faithful dog
Caleb		Hebrew	Faithful dog
Calhoun		American	From the narrow forest
Callum	Calum	Scottish, Irish	Dove
Calm		English	Tranquil
Calvin		Latin	Little bald one
Cam		Scottish	Crooked mouth
Cameron		Scottish	Crooked nose
Camillo		Italian	Ceremonial attendant/freedom
Camilo		French	Ceremonial attendant/freedom
Campbell		Scottish	Crooked mouth

Name	Alternative spellings	Origin	Meaning
Cane	Cain	Hebrew	Variant of Cain, son of Adam and Eve who killed his brother in the Bible
Caradoc		Cornish, Welsh	Lovable
Caradwg		Welsh	Lovable
Carbry		Irish	Charioteer
Carisio		Italian	Beauty, grace
Carl	Karl	German	Free man
Carlo		Italian	Manly
Carlos		Spanish	Manly
Carlyle		Place name	Town in the north of England
Carmel		Hebrew	Garden, orchard
Carrington		Anglo-Saxon	Place name and surname
Carson		American	Son who lives in a swamp
Cary		Welsh	Descendant of the dark one
Casey		Irish	Brave
Cash		English	Money
Caspar	Kaspar	Scandinavian	From the gem jasper
Caspian		Literary	*Prince Caspian* by C. S. Lewis
Cassidy		Irish	Clever
Cassio		Italian	Empty, hollow
Cassius		Latin	Empty, hollow
Castel		Spanish	Castle
Castor		Greek	One of the twin stars of the constellation Gemini

Name	Alternative spellings	Origin	Meaning
Caton		Spanish	Wise
Cecil		Latin	The blind one
Cedric	Cederic	Literary	*Ivanhoe* by Sir Walter Scott
Celio		Italian, Spanish	Heavenly
Cemal		Arabic	Perfect
Cesare		Italian	Hairy
Chacha		African	Strong
Chad		Anglo-Saxon	Warrior
Chale		Spanish	Boy
Chance		American	Gambler or lucky person
Chandan		Sanskrit	Of the sandalwood tree
Chandler		Anglo-Saxon	Candlemaker
Chandra		Sanskrit	Bright moon
Charles	Charlie, Chaz	French	Free man
Charlie	Chaz	French	Free man
Chase		French	Hunter
Chaz		American	From Charles, free man
Chester		Latin	Roman site or camp
Chevalier		French	Knight
Chibale		African	Kinship
Chimalsi		African	Proud
Chopin		Anglo-Saxon	Famous composer
Christhard		German	Brave Christian
Christian		Latin	Follower of Christ
Christophe		French	Bearer of Christ
Christopher		Greek	Bearer of Christ. Patron saint of travellers

Name	Alternative spellings	Origin	Meaning
Chuck		American	From Charles, free man
Churchill		English	From Winston Churchill
Ciaran		Welsh	Little dark one
Cicero		Latin	A chickpea or bean
Cid		Spanish	Lord
Cipriano		Italian	From Cyprus
Cirrus		Anglo-Saxon	A form of cloud
Clancy		Irish	Lively
Clarence		Latin	Clear, luminous
Clark	Clerk, Clarke	Latin	Clerk
Claude	Claud	Latin	Lame one
Claudio		Italian, Spanish	Lame one
Claus	Klaus	German	People's victory
Clay		American	From Clayton, town on clay land
Clayton		American	Town on clay land
Clement		Latin	Gentle, merciful
Cliff		Anglo-Saxon	Ford by the cliff
Clifford		Anglo-Saxon	Ford by the cliff
Clint		Anglo-Saxon	Town by the cliff
Clinton		Anglo-Saxon	Town by the cliff
Clive		Anglo-Saxon	Cliff by the river
Cloud		Anglo-Saxon	Water vapour in the sky
Clyde		Scottish	Warm
Cobain		American	Surname used as a first name. Surname of famous lead singer of Nirvana, Kurt Cobain

Name	Alternative spellings	Origin	Meaning
Cobalt		English	Silver grey metal
Cobar		Australian	Burnt earth
Cody	Codie	Irish	Cushion
Cohen	Kohen	Hebrew	From Kohen, meaning priest
Colbert		German	Famous protector
Colby		Anglo-Saxon	Dark
Coleman		Scottish, Irish	Dove
Colin		Irish	Young cub
Colm		Irish	Dove
Conall		Scottish	Strong wolf
Conan		Irish	Wolf, hound. Legendary Irish hero
Concordio		Italian	Agreeable
Conn		Irish	Chief, leader
Conor	Connor	Irish	Lover of hounds
Conrad		German	Brave advisor
Cooper		Anglo-Saxon	Barrel maker
Coorain		Australian	The wind
Corey	Cory	Irish	Lives near a hollow
Cormac		Irish	Raven's son
Cornelio		Italian, Spanish	From Cornelius, Roman soldier who became a Christian
Cornelius		Latin	Roman solider who became a Christian
Cortes		Spanish	Victorious
Cosimo		Italian	Order, decency
Cosmo		Greek	Harmony
Costanzo		Italian	Steadfast
Courtney		Anglo-Saxon	Courtier
Craig		Scottish	Rock

Name	Alternative spellings	Origin	Meaning
Creighton		Place name	Near the creek
Crispin		Latin	Curly haired
Cristiano		Italian	Follower of Christ
Cristo		Spanish	Follower of Christ
Cruze	Cruz	Spanish	Cross
Cupid		Latin	Son of Venus, a god of love
Curtis		Anglo-Saxon	Courteous
Cuthbert		Anglo-Saxon	Famous
Cyclone		Anglo-Saxon	Powerful and destructive weather system
Cyril		Greek	Lordly

D

Name	Alternative spellings	Origin	Meaning
Dadrian		American	From Adrian, dark, rich, from Hadria in Italy
Daffyd		Welsh	Beloved
Dahl		Scandinavian	Norwegian surname, name of Roald Dahl, famous children's author
Dai		Welsh	To shine
Dakota		American	US place name, American Indian tribe
Daktari		African	Healer
Daku		Australian	Sand
Daley		Irish	Gathering
Dalziel		Scottish	Small field
Damien	Damian, Damon	Greek	True friend
Dan		Hebrew	God is my judge
Daniel		Hebrew	God is my judge
Danil		Russian	God is my judge
Danny		Hebrew	God is my judge
Dante		Italian	Enduring
Darby		Place name	From Derby, deer settlement
Darcy		Irish	Dark
Darel		Australian	Blue sky
Darell		French	Beloved
Daric		Irish	Ruler of the people
Darien		Greek, Spanish	Wealthy Uncertain
Dario		Italian	He who possesses good things

Name	Alternative spellings	Origin	Meaning
Darius		Greek	He who possesses good things
Darragh		Irish, Scottish	Dark oak
Darren		Anglo-Saxon	Uncertain
Darrick		Irish, American	Ruler of the people. From Derrick, famous ruler
Darryl		French	From d'Ariele, a place in France
Dartagnan		French	Leader
Darwin		English	Australian city and name of famous scientist Charles Darwin
Dary		Irish	Wealthy
Dave		Hebrew	Beloved
David		Hebrew	Beloved
Davin		Welsh	Beloved
Davon		American	From Devon, English county
Deacon		Greek	Messenger
Dean		Latin	A soldier
Decca		Greek	Ten
Declan		Irish	Man of prayer
Dedalus		Greek	In mythology, builder of the Minotaur's labyrinth and Icarus' father
Deepak		Sanskrit	Like a lamp or light
Delaney		Irish	Son of the challenger
Dell		Anglo-Saxon	Hollow or valley
Demetrio		Italian	From Demeter, Greek goddess of agriculture
Demetrius		Spanish	From Demeter, Greek goddess of agriculture
Dempsey		Irish	Proud

Name	Alternative spellings	Origin	Meaning
Denby		Anglo-Saxon	From the Danish settlement
Dennis		Greek	Wild. Lover of wine
Denton		Anglo-Saxon	Settlement in the valley
Denver		Place name	US city
Denzel		Cornish	Cornish surname and place name
Deo		Greek	God-like
Derain		Australian	Of the mountains
Derek		German	Ruler of the people
Dermot		Irish	Free of envy
Desidirio		Italian, Spanish	Desire
Desmond		Irish	Man from south Munster
Dev		Sanskrit	Godlike
Devante		Spanish	From a Spanish aristocratic surname
Devdan		Sanskrit	The gift of the gods
Devin		Irish	Poet
Devlyn		Irish	Brave
Devon		Place name	English county
Dewey		American	Welsh surname and place name. From David, beloved
Dexter		Latin	Right handed, dexterous
Dheran		Australian	A gully
Diallo		African	Bold
Diarmaid		Irish	Free of envy
Didier		French	Desired
Diego		Italian, Spanish	Teacher
Dieter		German	People's army
Diezel Ky		Celebrity child	(Toni Braxton and Keri Lewis)

Name	Alternative spellings	Origin	Meaning
Digby		Anglo-Saxon	Ditch town
Diggory		French	Lost
Dillan	Dillon	Welsh	Celtic god associated with the sea
Dima		Russian	From Demeter, Greek goddess of agriculture
Dimitri		Russian	From Demeter, Greek goddess of agriculture
Dinesh		Sanskrit	The lord of the day
Dirk		American	From Derek
Dmitri		Russian	From Demeter, Greek goddess of agriculture
Dobby		Literary	House elf in the Harry Potter books
Dolph		German	From Adolph, noble wolf
Domenico		Italian	Belonging to God
Domhnall		Scottish	World ruler
Dominic		Latin	Belonging to God
Dominique		French	Belonging to God
Donal		Scottish	World ruler
Donald	Don	Scottish	World ruler
Donatien		French	Gift
Donovan		Irish	Dark-haired chief
Dorado		Spanish	Swordfish, a constellation
Dorak		Australian	Lively
Dorian		Literary	*The Picture of Dorian Gray* by Oscar Wilde
Dougal		Scottish	Dark stranger
Douglas	Doug	Scottish	Dark river
Doyle		Irish	Dark stranger
Draco		Latin	Dragon. A constellation
Drake		Irish	Dark stranger

Name	Alternative spellings	Origin	Meaning
Drew		Greek	Manly
Dudley		Anglo-Saxon	The people's meadow
Duke		American	Nobleman
Duncan		Scottish	Brown warrior
Dunmor	Dunmore	Scottish	Great hill fortress
Durand		American	Enduring
Durante		Italian	Steadfast
Durwin		Anglo-Saxon	Friend of the deer
Durwyn		Anglo-Saxon	Friend of the deer
Dustin	Dusty	Anglo-Saxon	Dusty town
Dwayne		Irish	Dark
Dwight		American	Wine lover
Dwyer		Irish	Dark
Dylan	Dillon, Dylon	Welsh	Celtic god Dillan, associated with the sea

E

Name	Alternative spellings	Origin	Meaning
Eagle		English	Bird of prey
Eamon	Eamonn, Eammon	Irish	Wealthy guardian
Earl	Earle	Anglo-Saxon	Nobleman
Ebbo		German	Boar
Ebenezer		Hebrew	Foundation stone. First name of Charles Dickens' mean-spirited Scrooge
Eberardo		Italian	Strong as a wild boar
Eddison	Eddie	Anglo-Saxon	Son of Edward
Eden		Hebrew	Pleasure
Edgar		Anglo-Saxon	Lucky spearman
Edilio		Italian	Like a statue
Edmondo		Italian	Wealthy guardian
Edmund	Edmond	Anglo-Saxon	Prosperous protector
Édouard		French	Wealthy guardian
Eduardo		Italian	Wealthy guardian
Edward	Ted, Ed, Eddy	Anglo-Saxon	Wealthy guardian
Edwin	Edwyn	Anglo-Saxon	Prosperous friend
Efrain		Spanish	Fruitful
Eldon		Anglo-Saxon	Foreign hill
Eldrid		Anglo-Saxon	Old and wise advisor
Eldwyn		Anglo-Saxon	Old and wise friend
Elewa		African	Intelligent
Eli		American	From Elijah, the Lord is my God, biblical prophet
Elia	Eliyah	Italian	My God is Yaweh, biblical prophet
Eligio		Italian	Chosen

Name	Alternative spellings	Origin	Meaning
Elijah	Elia, Eliyah	Hebrew	My God is Yaweh, biblical prophet
Eliot	Elliot	Hebrew	Anglo-Saxon surname, adapted from Elijah
Ellis		Hebrew	God is my Lord
Ellison		Hebrew	God is my Lord
Elmer		Anglo-Saxon	Noble
Elton		Anglo-Saxon	Ella's town
Elvis		Anglo-Saxon	All wise
Emanuele	Emmanuele	Italian	God is with us
Emerson		American	Surname
Emil		Latin	Ingratiating
Émile		French	Rival
Emilio		Italian, Spanish	Rival
Emir		Arabic	Charming prince
Emmanuel		Hebrew	God is with us
Emmet		Anglo-Saxon	Hard working
Emmett		American	Hard working, strong
Emrys		Welsh	Immortal
Ennio		Italian	Predestined, favoured by God
Enoch		Hebrew	Teacher
Enrico		Italian	Ruler of the home
Enrique		Spanish	Ruler of the home
Erasmus		Greek	Worthy of love
Ercole		Italian	Glory of Hera (after Hercules, mythical Greek hero)
Eric		Anglo-Saxon	Eternal ruler
Erik	Eric, Eirik	Scandinavian	Eternal ruler
Erin		Irish	From Ireland
Erland		Scandinavian	Stranger
Ernst		German	Serious business. Fight to the death

Name	Alternative spellings	Origin	Meaning
Eros		Greek	God of love in myth, also known as Cupid
Errol		Latin	To wander
Esme		French	Handsome
Esmond		Anglo-Saxon	Wealthy protector
Esteban		Spanish	Crown
Etan		Hebrew	Strong or long-lived
Ethan		Hebrew	Strong or long-lived
Étienne		French	Crown
Euan	Eoghan, Ewan	Scottish	Born of the yew
Eugene		Greek	Well born
Eustace		Greek	Steadfast
Evan		Welsh	God is gracious
Evelyn		Anglo-Saxon	Desired
Everley		American	Singing
Evert		German	Boar, strong, hardy
Ewan	Eoghan, Euan	Scottish	Born of the yew
Eze		African	King
Ezio		Italian	Eagle
Ezra		Hebrew	Strong

F

Name	Alternative spellings	Origin	Meaning
Fabian		Latin	Bean grower
Fabio		Italian	Bean grower
Fable		English	Story with a lesson
Fabrizio		Italian	Craftsman
Faddei		Russian	Heart
Fadil		Arabic	The generous or distinguished one
Fahim		African	Learned
Fairfax		English	Warm
Faisal		Arabic	A wise judge
Falcon		English	Bird of prey
Fargo		American	US place name
Farhani		African	Happy
Farid		Arabic	Unique, unrivalled
Farley		Anglo-Saxon	The far meadow
Farook		Arabic	One who can distinguish right from wrong
Farquar	Farquart	French	Masculine
Farrell		Irish	Hero
Fausto		Italian, Spanish	Lucky, fortunate one
Faustus		Latin	Lucky, fortunate one
Faysal		Arabic	A wise judge
Fearghal		Irish	Brave man
Federico		Italian, Spanish	Peaceful ruler
Fedot		Russian	Given to God
Felipe		Spanish	Horse lover
Felix		Latin	Happy and prosperous
Feofilakt		Russian	Guarded by God
Feofilart		Russian	Guarded by God
Ferapont		Russian	Servant

Name	Alternative spellings	Origin	Meaning
Ferdinand		Anglo-Saxon	Brave peacemaker
Ferdinando		Italian, Spanish	Brave peacemaker
Ferghus		Irish	Properous
Fergus		Irish	Prosperous
Ferguson		Irish	Brave, excellent
Fernando		Spanish	Brave leader
Feroz		Arabic	Victorious and successful
Ferran		Arabic	Baker
Ferrari		Italian	Italian surname meaning blacksmith, also famous supercar
Ferruccio		Italian	Iron man
Festus		Latin	Happy
Fidel		Latin	Faithful
Fidenzio		Italian	Faithful
Fife		Scottish	Bright-eyed
Figaro		Latin	Daring, cunning
Filiberto		Italian	Illustrious
Filippo		Italian	Lover of horses
Filius		Latin	Son
Finbar	Fin, Fynbar	Irish	Fair haired
Findlay	Finlay, Finley	Irish, Scottish	Fair-haired hero
Finn		Irish	Fair
Finnegan		Irish	Fair
Fiorello		Italian	Flourishing
Fiorenzo		Italian	Flourishing
Firdos		Arabic	Paradise
Fire		Anglo-Saxon	Flames
Firenze		Latin	City of Florence, Italy
Fitzgerald		German	Son of the spear ruler
Flame		Anglo-Saxon	Flicker from a fire
Flannagan		Irish	Red-head
Flavio		Italian	Blonde, golden

Name	Alternative spellings	Origin	Meaning
Floyd		Anglo-Saxon	Grey or white haired
Flynn		Irish	Son of the red-headed man
Foley		Anglo-Saxon	Creative
Foma		Russian	Twin
Ford		Anglo-Saxon	Lives near the ford
Forest		Anglo-Saxon	Large area of trees
Fosco		Italian	Dark
Fowler		Anglo-Saxon	Hunter
Fran		French	From François, Frenchman
Francesco		Italian	From France
Francis	Frances, Fran	Latin	Free man/from France
Francisco		Spanish	From France, free
Franco		Italian	From France
François		French	From France
Frank		Anglo-Saxon	Frenchman
Frankie		Latin	From France/free man
Franklin		Anglo-Saxon	Freeman who owns property
Franz		German	Frenchman
Fraser	Frasier	French	Strawberry
Frasier	Fraser	French	Strawberry
Fred		Anglo-Saxon	Brave peacemaker
Freddie		Anglo-Saxon	Brave peacemaker
Frédéric		French	Brave peacemaker
Frederick	Fred, Freddie	Anglo-Saxon	Peace
Frederik		German	Peace, power
Free		English	At liberty
Freeman		Anglo-Saxon	Free man
Friedrich		German	Peace, power
Fritz		German	Peace, power
Frode		Scandinavian	Knowing
Fulbright		German	Brilliant, bright
Furio		Italian	Lively one

G

Name	Alternative spellings	Origin	Meaning
Gabe		Hebrew	God is my strength
Gabrian		Hebrew	God is my strength
Gabriel	Gabriele	Hebrew	God is my strength
Galen		Greek	Calm
Galeno		Spanish, Italian	From Galilee
Gallagher		Irish	Helpful
Gallileo		Italian	From famous scientist Gallilei Gallileo
Gamal		Arabic	Camel
Gambero		Spanish	Hooligan
Ganan		Australian	From the west
Gandhi		Sanskrit	Sun
Gandolfo		Italian	Wolf, warrior
Ganesh		Sanskrit	The Hindu god of wisdom
Garcia		Spanish	Strong
Gareth		Welsh	Gentle
Garsah		Russian	Honour
Gary		Welsh	Gentle
Gaspare		Italian	Respected teacher
Gautama		Sanskrit	The name of the Buddha
Gavin		Welsh	White falcon
Gavriel		Hebrew	God is my strength
Gavril		Russian	Strength of God
Gawain		Welsh	White falcon
Gelar		Australian	A brother
Gene		Greek	Noble
Gennadi		Russian	Noble
Gennaro		Italian	Dedicated to the god Janus
Geno		Italian	Spontaneous
Gentil		Spanish	Charming

Name	Alternative spellings	Origin	Meaning
Geoff		Anglo-Saxon	Peaceful
Geoffrey		Anglo-Saxon	Peaceful
George	Jorge	Greek	Farmer
Georges	Jorges	Greek	From the farm
Georgie		Greek	Farmer
Gerald		Anglo-Saxon	Brave with a spear
Geraldo		Italian	Brave with a spear
Gerard		Anglo-Saxon	Brave with a spear
Gérard		French	Brave with a spear
Gere		English	Dramatic
Germain		French	From Germany
Geronimo		Italian	Sacred name. A famous Apache chief
Gervaise		French	Man of honour
Gethin		Welsh	Dusky
Ghalib		African	Winner
Ghassan		Arabic	Youthful
Giacomo		Italian	He who replaces
Giancarlo		Italian	God is gracious, strong
Gianetto		Italian	God is gracious
Gianfranco		Italian	God is gracious/ free man, from France
Gianni		Italian	God is gracious
Gideon	Gidon	Hebrew	Tree cutter
Gidon	Gideon	Hebrew	Tree cutter
Gil		Hebrew	Eternal joy
Gilderoy		Latin	Golden king
Gildo		Italian	Brave one
Giles		Greek	Young goat
Gili		Hebrew	Eternal joy
Gillespie		Scottish	Humble
Gilli		Hebrew	Eternal joy

Name	Alternative spellings	Origin	Meaning
Gilroy		Scottish	Serves the king
Gino		Italian	God is gracious
Ginton		Arabic	Garden
Giorgio		Italian	Farmer
Giovanni		Italian	God is gracious
Gladwyn		Anglo-Saxon	Light of heart
Glen	Glenn	Scottish	Secluded valley
Glyn	Glynn	Welsh	Secluded valley
Godfrey		German	God's peace
Godric		Anglo-Saxon	Power of God
Goldie		Anglo-Saxon	Precious metal
Gomez		Spanish	From Spanish surname meaning man
Gopal		Sanskrit	The cowherd
Gordon		Anglo-Saxon	Hill near the meadow
Govinda		Sanskrit	A cowherd
Gowan		Welsh	Pure
Graeme	Graham, Grahame	Scottish	Grand home
Graham		Anglo-Saxon	Grand home
Grant		Scottish	Large
Grégoire		French	Watchman
Gregorio		Italian	Watchman
Gregory	Greg, Gregor	Greek	Watchful
Griffin		Greek	Mythical animal: half eagle, half lion
Grigor		Russian	Watchful
Guido		Italian	Guide
Guillaume		Anglo-Saxon	Strong protector
Guillermo		Spanish	Strong protector
Giuseppe		Italian	God will add
Gunne		Scandinavian	Strife

Name	Alternative spellings	Origin	Meaning
Gunther		German	Army of strife
Gustav		Scandinavian	Staff of the Goths
Guthne		Irish	Heroic
Guy		Latin	Guide
Gwithyen		Cornish	From St Gwithian

H

Name	Alternative spellings	Origin	Meaning
Haamid		African	Grateful
Habib		Arabic	The beloved one
Hadi		Arabic	A guide or leader
Hafiz		Arabic	The guardian
Hagrid		Greek	Giant in Greek mythology
Hail		Anglo-Saxon	Ice that falls like rain
Hakim		Arabic	Wise and judicious
Haley		Irish	Innovator
Halvard		Scandinavian	Strong defender
Hamal		Arabic	As gentle as a lamb
Hamid		Arabic	The thankful one
Hamilton		Anglo-Saxon	Grassy hill
Hamish		Scottish	He who replaces
Hamlet		Literary	*Hamlet* by William Shakespeare
Hani		Arabic	The contented one
Hank		American	From Henry, home ruler
Hansel		German	God is gracious
Harald		Scandinavian	Army leader
Hari		Sanskrit	He who removes evil
Harold		Scandinavian	Army ruler
Harrison		Anglo-Saxon	Son of Harry
Harry		Anglo-Saxon	Ruler of home
Hartley	Hartly	Anglo-Saxon	Wanderer
Harvey		Scottish, Irish	Eager for battle
Hasim		Arabic	The decisive one
Hassan		Arabic	Handsome
Havard		Scandinavian	Strong protector
Hayward		Anglo-Saxon	Keeper of the field
Heath		Anglo-Saxon	Moorland

Name	Alternative spellings	Origin	Meaning
Hector		Greek	To hold fast. Mythical hero of Troy
Heinrich		German	Ruler of the home
Heinz		German	Ruler of the home
Helmut		German	Protective spirit
Henderson		Anglo-Saxon	Son of Henry
Henri		French	Ruler of the home
Henry		Anglo-Saxon	Ruler of the home
Herbert		German	Famous army
Hercules		Greek	Mythical hero of immense strength
Hermann		German	Army of men
Hermes		Greek	Messenger of the gods
Hernando		Spanish	Brave peacemaker
Hevan		Hebrew	An older form of the word 'heaven'
Hilary	Hillary	Latin	To rejoice
Hilton		Anglo-Saxon	From the hill town
Hobart		American	Ploughmans hill
Hockney		Anglo-Saxon	Surname, notably of artist David Hockney
Holden		Anglo-Saxon	Deep valley. Hero of J. D. Salinger's *The Catcher in the Rye*
Holder		Anglo-Saxon	Possessor of real estate
Honoré		French	Honourable
Hopper		Celebrity child	(Sean Penn and Robin Wright)
Horace		Latin	An hour
Horatio		Latin	An hour
Houston		American	US city
Howe		German	High minded

Name	Alternative spellings	Origin	Meaning
Hubert		German	Famous heart
Hugh		Anglo-Saxon	Bright mind
Hugo		German	Heart, mind, spirit
Humbert		German	Famous warrior
Humphrey		German	Peacemaker
Hurley		Irish	Sea tide
Hurricane		Anglo-Saxon	Powerful weather system
Hussain	Hussein	Arabic	The handsome little one
Huxley		Anglo-Saxon	Outdoors man

I

Name	Alternative spellings	Origin	Meaning
Iago		Spanish	The supplanter
Iain	Ian	Scottish	God is gracious
Ian	Iain	Scottish	God is gracious
Ice		Anglo-Saxon	Frozen water
Ichabod		Hebrew	Slim
Igor		Russian	Bow army
Ilya		Russian	Elijah
Imam		Arabic	One who believes in God
Iman		African	Faith
Immanuel		Hebrew	God is with us
Indra		Sanskrit	The God of the sky
Ingelbert		German	Combative
Ingram		Anglo-Saxon	Angel
Innis		Irish	Isolated
Ioan	Euan, Ewan	Welsh	Youthful
Ira		Hebrew	Cautious
Irwin	Irwyn	Anglo-Saxon	Sea friend
Isaac		Hebrew	Laughter
Isidro		Spanish	Gift of the godess Isis
Israel		Hebrew	God's prince
Ivan		Russian	God is gracious
Ivar		Scandinavian	Archer
Ivor		Anglo-Saxon	Archer's bow
Izaak		Polish	Laughter
Izzy		Hebrew	Friendly

J

Name	Alternative spellings	Origin	Meaning
Jaafar		African	Small river
Jabir		Arabic	The comforter
Jacca		Cornish	God is gracious
Jack		Anglo-Saxon	God is gracious
Jackie		Irish, Scottish	God is gracious
Jackson		Anglo-Saxon	Son of Jack
Jacob		Hebrew	The supplanter
Jacques		French	The supplanter
Jaden	Jayden, Jadon, Jaydon	Hebrew	God has heard
Jagdish		Sanskrit	The ruler of the world
Jagger		Anglo-Saxon	Carter
Jago		Cornish	The supplanter
Jaguar		Spanish	Fast
Jaimie		Anglo-Saxon	The supplanter
Jake		Hebrew	The supplanter
Jaleel		Arabic	Great
Jalil		Arabic	Majestic
Jamal		Arabic	The handsome one
James	Jamie	Anglo-Saxon	The supplanter
Jared		Hebrew	Descending
Jarrah		Australian	A type of tree
Jarrett		Hebrew	Confident
Jarvis		Anglo-Saxon	Servant with a spear
Jason		Greek	Healer. Also mythical Greek hero
Jasper		Anglo-Saxon	Semi-precious red gem
Java		Place name	Indonesian island
Javier		Spanish	The new house
Jaycee		American	From the initials J. C.

Name	Alternative spellings	Origin	Meaning
Jayden	Jaydon, Jaden, Jadon	Hebrew	God has heard
Jazz		American	From Jason, healer, mythical Greek hero, or Jasper, semi-precious red gem
Jean		French	God is gracious
Jedadiah	Jed, Jedd	Hebrew	Beloved by God
Jedd		Hebrew	Beloved by God
Jedi		Hebrew	Beloved by God
Jefferson		American	Son of Jeffrey
Jeffrey	Geoffrey	Anglo-Saxon	Peaceful
Jem	Jemmy	Literary	*To Kill a Mockingbird* by Harper Lee, *Jamaica Inn* by Daphne du Maurier
Jerara		Australian	Falling water
Jeremiah		Hebrew	God will uplift
Jeremias		Spanish	God will uplift
Jeremy	Jez, Jem	Anglo-Saxon	God will uplift
Jermaine		French	Brother
Jermajesty		Celebrity child	(Jermaine Jackson)
Jerome		Greek	Sacred name
Jerral		American	From Gerald, brave with a spear
Jerrett		Hebrew	Confident
Jesse	Jess	Hebrew	Wealthy/God's gift
Jesus		Hebrew	Jehova is salvation
Jet		Latin	Black
Jethro		Hebrew	Overflowing or abundance
Jevon		Anglo-Saxon	Young
Jim	Jimmy	Anglo-Saxon	From James, he who replaces
Jirra		Australian	A kangaroo

Name	Alternative spellings	Origin	Meaning
Jitender		Sanskrit	The powerful conqueror
Joachim		Hebrew	Established by God
Joaquim		Hebrew	Established by God
Jock		Scottish	God is gracious
Joe	Jo	Hebrew	Shortened version of Joseph
Joel		Hebrew	The Lord is God
Johanne	Johan, Johannes	Scandinavian	God is gracious
John	Jon	Hebrew	God is gracious
Jonah		Hebrew	Dove
Jonas		Hebrew	Dove
Jonathan	Jonathon	Hebrew	Gift of God
Jonte		American	God is gracious
Jools	Jules	Anglo-Saxon	Young
Jordan		Hebrew	To flow down or descend
Jorell		American	Mighty spearman
Jorge		Spanish	Farmer
Jose		Spanish	God will add
Joseph		Hebrew	God will add
Josh		Hebrew	God is salvation
Joshua		Hebrew	God is salvation
Joss		Hebrew	God is salvation
Jove		Latin	Roman god of the sky
Jowan		Cornish	God is gracious
Juan		Spanish	God is gracious
Jud		Hebrew	Praised
Judas		Hebrew	Praised. Disciple who betrayed Christ
Judd	Jud	Latin	Secretive
Jude		Hebrew	Praised
Judge		English	To form an opinion, or person who presides over a court of law

Name	Alternative spellings	Origin	Meaning
Jules		Latin	Youthful
Julian	Julien	French	Youthful
Julius		Latin	Youthful
Justin		Latin	Just or true
Justus		Latin	Fair
Jyotis		Sanskrit	Light

K

Name	Alternative spellings	Origin	Meaning
Kacy		American	From Casey, brave
Kadin		Arabic	Friend
Kadir		Arabic	Powerful
Kai		Pacific Islands	Good looking
Kale		American	Healthy
Kalid		Arabic	Eternal
Kalil		Arabic	Good friend
Kama		Sanskrit	The golden one
Kamal		Arabic	Perfect
Kamil		Arabic	Perfect
Kane		Irish	Tribute
Karan		Sanskrit	A warrior
Kari		Australian	Smoke
Karim		Arabic	Noble and generous
Karl		Russian	Manly
Karl		German	Free man
Karsten		German	Christian
Kasey		Irish	Brave
Kasim		Arabic	One who shares or distributes
Kaspar		Scandinavian	From the semi-precious gem, jasper
Kateb		Arabic	Scribe
Kauri		Pacific Islands	A kind of tree
Kay		Welsh	Joy
Kazimir		Russian	To destroy greatness
Keagan		Irish	Little fire
Kean		Irish	Handsome
Keanan		Irish	Ancient
Keane		German	Attractive
Keanu		Pacific Islands	Cool breeze over the mountain
Kearney		Irish	Sparkling

Name	Alternative spellings	Origin	Meaning
Keats		Literary	Surname of the Romantic poet
Kedar		Arabic	Powerful
Keefe		Irish	Handsome
Keegan		Irish	Little fire
Keenan		Irish	Ancient
Keith		Welsh	Of the forest
Kelly		Irish	Warrior
Kelsey		Scandinavian	Unique
Kelvin		Irish	From the narrow river
Kemal		Arabic	Perfect
Ken		Irish	Handsome
Kendall		Anglo-Saxon	Shy
Kendrick		Irish	Royal ruler
Kennedy		Irish	Ugly head. Surname of US President, John F. Kennedy
Kenneth		Irish	Handsome
Kent		Place name	English county
		Welsh	Bright
Keoni		Pacific Islands	The righteous one
Kevern		Cornish	From St Kevern
Kevin		Irish	Little gentle one
Khalid		Arabic	Eternal
Khalif		Arabic	Successor
Khalil		Arabic	A friend
Kid		American	Slang for child
Kieran		Irish	Little dark one
Kim		Anglo-Saxon	Warrior chief
King		Anglo-Saxon	Ruler
Kingsley		Anglo-Saxon	From the king's meadow
Kipp		Anglo-Saxon	From the pointed hill
Kiran		Sanskrit	A ray of light
Kirby		Anglo-Saxon	From the church town
Kirwyn		Welsh	Dark skinned

Name	Alternative spellings	Origin	Meaning
Kit		Greek	Bearer of Christ
Klaud		Latin	The lame one
Knox		Anglo-Saxon	Bold
Knut		Scandinavian	Knot, a short, stout man
Kofi		African	Born on Friday. First name of Nobel Peace Prize winner, Kofi Annan
Kolet		Australian	A dove
Kolya		Russian	Victory of the people
Konrad		German	Brave advisor
Koorong		Australian	A canoe
Kosey		African	Lion
Krishna		Sanskrit	Dark, black
Krispin	Krispen	Latin	Curly haired
Kristian		Scandinavian	Follower of Christ
Kristopher		Greek	Bearer of Christ
Kulan		Australian	A possom
Kumar		Sanskrit	Boy
Kupe		Pacific Islands	A heroic explorer
Kurt		German	Brave advisor
Kyd		Celebrity child	(David Duchovny and Téa Leoni)
Kyle		Scottish	Narrow channel
Kyzer		American	Wild spirit

L

Name	Alternative spellings	Origin	Meaning
Lacy		Latin	From the Roman villa
Lai		Sanskrit	The beloved one
Lakshman		Sanskrit	Lucky
Lamberto		Italian	Famous in his country
Lance		Anglo-Saxon	Knight's attendant
Lando		Italian	Land, earth
Lane		Anglo-Saxon	From a narrow lane
Langley		Anglo-Saxon	Lives by a meadow
Lani		Pacific Islands	The sky
Larry		Latin	Crowned with laurels
Latif		Arabic	Kind and gentle
Laurence	Lawrence	Latin	Crowned with laurels
Laurent		French	Crowned with laurels
Laurie		Latin	Crowned with laurels
Leaf		Anglo-Saxon	Foliage
Leander		Greek	The lion man
Lee		Anglo-Saxon	From the meadow
Leighton		Anglo-Saxon	From the meadow farm
Leith		Scottish	Wide river
Lemony		Literature	From Lemony Snicket: pen name of author of *A Series of Unfortunate Events*
Lennon		Irish	Lover, sweetheart
Lennox		Scottish	From the place of many elm trees
Leo		Italian, Latin	Lion
Léon		Latin	Like a lion
Leonardo		Italian, Spanish	Like a lion
Leone		Italian	Lion

Name	Alternative spellings	Origin	Meaning
Leopold		Italian	He who is distinguished
Leroy		French	The king
Lesley	Leslie	Scottish	From the grey fortress
Lestat		Literary	*Vampire Chronicles* by Anne Rice
Lester		Anglo-Saxon	From the army camp
Levi		Hebrew	Joined or united
Lewis		Anglo-Saxon	Famous fighter
Lewyth		Cornish	Ruler
Liam		Irish	Strong protector
Liberio		Italian	Independent
Libero		Italian	Independent
Lincoln		Welsh	Lake on a hill ridge. Name of US President Abraham Lincoln
Lindsey		Anglo-Saxon	Lincoln's marsh
Linford		Anglo-Saxon	From the lime tree ford
Linus		Greek	Blond haired
Lionel		Latin	A lion
Lisandro		Italian	Free man
Ljluka		Sanskrit	An owl
Llewelyn		Welsh	Like a lion
Lloyd		Welsh	Grey hair
Logan		Irish	Lives by the hollow
London		Place name	Capital of the UK
Lorenzo		Italian	From Laurentum, an ancient Roman city
Lorimer		Latin	Home is water
Louis		French	Famous fighter
Lowan		Australian	A type of bird
Luc		French	Born in the light
Luca		Italian	Born in the light
Lucas		French	Born in the light

Name	Alternative spellings	Origin	Meaning
Lucian		Latin	Born in the light
Luciano		Italian	Born in the light
Lucio		Italian, Spanish	Born in the light
Lucius		Latin	Born in the light
Ludo		Latin	I play
Ludwig		German	Famous warrior
Luigi		Italian	Famous fighter
Luis		Spanish	Famous fighter
Luka		Russian	From Luke, born in the light
Luke		Greek	Born in the light. One of Christ's apostles
Lupus		Latin	Wolf, a constellation
Luther		German	People's army
Lyle		Scottish	Loyal
Lyman	Leyman	Anglo-Saxon	From the meadow
Lyndon		Anglo-Saxon	Lives by the linden tree
Lynn		Welsh	From the waterfall
Lynshawn		American	Lyn and Shawn
Lyon		Place name	French city
Lyov		Russian	Lion
Lysander		Greek	The liberator
Lyulf		German	Combative

M

Name	Alternative spellings	Origin	Meaning
Maalik		African	Experienced
Mac		Scottish, Irish	Son
Mack		Scottish, Irish	Son
Mackenzie		Scottish, Irish	Son of Coinnich, 'comely'
Macy		French	Weapon
Maddox		Welsh	Benefactor's son
Magic		English	An extraordinary or mystical influence
Magnus		Greek	The great one
Mahatma		Sanskrit	Great soul
Mahendra		Sanskrit	The God of the sky
Mahesh		Sanskrit	A great ruler
Mahmood		Arabic	Praiseworthy
Mahomet		Arabic	Praiseworthy
Mahoney		Irish	Bear
Majid		Arabic	The illustrious one
Maka		Australian	A camp fire
Malcolm		Scottish	Servant
Malik		Arabic	The master or king
Mallory		Anglo-Saxon	Military advisor
Malone		Irish	Church-goer
Mandela		African	Name of Nobel Peace Prize winner Nelson Mandela
Manfred		Anglo-Saxon	Peaceful hero
Mani		Sanskrit	A gem
Mansoor		Arabic	Victorious
Manu		Pacific Islands	Man of the birds
Manuel		Italian, Spanish	God is with us
Marama		Pacific Islands	Moon man

Name	Alternative spellings	Origin	Meaning
Marcel		French	From Mars, god of war
Marcello		Italian	From Mars, god of war
Marco		Italian, Spanish	From Mars, god of war
Marcus		Latin	From Mars, god of war, warrior
Mariano		Italian	Devoted to the Virgin Mary
Mario		Italian	Devoted to the Virgin Mary
Mark	Marc	Latin	From Mars, god of war, warrior
Marley		Anglo-Saxon	Pleasant wood
Marlon		Anglo-Saxon	Little hawk
Marmion		French	A monkey, naughty child
Marron		Australian	A leaf
Martin	Martyn	Latin	From Mars, god of war, warrior
Martino		Italian	Warrior
Marvin	Marvyn	Anglo-Saxon	Lives by the sea
Massimo		Italian	Large
Masud		Arabic	The fortunate one
Matareka		Pacific Islands	One with a smiling face
Matari		Australian	A man
Matthew	Mathew	Hebrew	Gift of Jehova
Matthieu		French	Gift of Jehova
Maui		Pacific Islands	Legendary hero
Maurice		Latin	Dark skinned, Moorish
Maverick		American	A rebel
Mawgan		Cornish	Mighty prince

Name	Alternative spellings	Origin	Meaning
Maxwell		Anglo-Saxon	Lives by the spring
Mayer		Latin	Greater
Maynard		Anglo-Saxon	Exceptionally brave and strong
McCartney		Scottish	Son of Cartney
Melbourne		Anglo-Saxon	From the mill stream
Melville		French	Mill town
Melvin		Irish	Armoured chief
Memphis		Place name	US city
Meredith		Welsh	Protector from the sea
Merlin		Welsh	Sea hill
Merrill		French	Little famous one
Merton		Anglo-Saxon	Sea town
Michael	Mike	Hebrew	Who is like God
Michel		French	In God's likeness
Michelangelo		Italian	Like God, an angel
Micky	Mickey	Hebrew	Who is like God
Miguel		Spanish	Like God
Mikhail		Russian	Like God
Mikula		Russian	Victory of the people
Milan		Place name	Italian city
Milburn		Anglo-Saxon	Mill stream
Miles		Latin	A soldier
Milton		Anglo-Saxon	Mill town
Minty		American	From the herb, mint
Misha		Russian	Like God
Mohammed		Arabic	The praised one
Mohan		Sanskrit	The bewitching one
Mohinder		Sanskrit	The God of the sky
Money		American	Cash

Name	Alternative spellings	Origin	Meaning
Monroe		Irish, Scottish	Mouth of the River Rotha
Montana		Place name	US state
Montgomery		Anglo-Saxon	From the wealthy man's mountain
Monti		Australian	A stork
Moore		French	Dark stranger
Morell		French	Secretive
Morgan		Scottish	Sea warrior
Morris		Latin	Dark skinned, Moorish
Morrissey		Anglo-Saxon	Choice of the sea
Morten		Scandinavian	Warrior
Morton		Anglo-Saxon	Town by the moor
Moses		Hebrew	Drawn from water
Moswen		African	Pale
Mowan		Australian	The sun
Mubarak		Arabic	Fortunate
Muhammad	Muhammed, Mohammed	Arabic	The praised one
Mukhtar		Arabic	The chosen one
Mundungus		Latin	Rubbish
Mungo		Scottish	Lovable
Murdoch		Scottish	Sea farer
Murray		Scottish	Lord of the sea
Muzio		Italian	Silent, quiet
Myles		Latin	A soldier
Mylo		Latin	A soldier

N

Name	Alternative spellings	Origin	Meaning
Naasir		African	Defender
Nabil		Arabic	Noble
Nadir		Arabic	Precious, rare
Nambur		Australian	A tea tree
Nanda		Sanskrit	Joy
Nanji		African	Safe
Napolean		German	Domineering
Narayan		Sanskrit	The son of man
Narciso		Italian	Self love
Nardu		Australian	A type of plant
Narendra		Sanskrit	The mighty man
Narrah		Australian	The sea
Nasir		Arabic	The helper
Nassir		Arabic	Protector
Nassor		African	Victorious
Nat		Hebrew	The gift of God
Natal		Spanish	Born at Christmas
Nathan		Hebrew	The gift of God
Navarro		Spanish	Wild spirit
Neal	Neale	Irish	Champion
Ned		Anglo-Saxon	Wealthy guardian
Neil		Scottish	Champion
Nellie		Anglo-Saxon	From Nelson, singing
Nelson		English	Son of Neil
Nemo		Latin	No name, nobody
Neo		Greek	New
Nereo		Italian	Great swimmer
Nero		Latin	Dark
Neron		Spanish	Strong
Nestor		Greek	Wisdom
Nevada		Spanish	Snow-capped
Neville		French	From the new town
Newbie		American	Beginner

Name	Alternative spellings	Origin	Meaning
Newlin		Welsh	Able
Newton		Anglo-Saxon	From the new town
Niall		Irish	Champion
Nicholas	Nick, Nicky, Nicolas	Greek	Victory of the people
Nicolas		French	Victory of the people
Niels	Nils	Scandinavian	Victory of the people
Nigel		Latin	Dark, black haired
Nike		Greek	Winning
Nikita		Russian	Unconquerable
Niklaus		Scandinavian	Victory of the people
Nikolai		Russian	Victory of the people
Nimrod		Latin	Valiant/great hunter
Nino		Italian	Handsome
Nioka		Australian	Hills
Nirvana		Sanskrit	In Buddhism, Nirvana is a blissful spiritual state of clarity and compassion
Nissan		Hebrew	Omen
Nixon		Anglo-Saxon	Audacious
Noah		Hebrew	Rest, peace
Noe		French	Rest, peace
Noël		French	Christmas
Nolan		Irish	Noble
Norbert		German	Famous one from the north
Nordin		Scandinavian	Handsome
Norman		Anglo-Saxon	Norseman
Norton		Anglo-Saxon	From the north town
Norville		French	Northern town
Norward		Anglo-Saxon	Guardian of the north
Nuri		Arabic	Fire
Nyle	Niall	Irish	Champion

O

Name	Alternative spellings	Origin	Meaning
Oakley		Anglo-Saxon	From the oak meadow
Oberon		Literary	*A Midsummer Night's Dream* by William Shakespeare
Ocean		Greek	Immense
Ochre		English	Brown, yellow
Octavius		Latin	The eighth born
Odin		Anglo-Saxon	God of all
Odongo		African	Second of twins
Ogden		Anglo-Saxon	From the oak valley
Ola		Scandinavian	Ancestor, heir
Olaf		Scandinavian	Ancestor, heir
Oleg		Russian	Successful
Olindo		Italian	From Olinthos, in Greece
Oliver	Ollie	Latin	Of the olive tree, peaceful
Olivero		Italian	Olive tree
Olivier		French	Olive tree
Oman		Scandinavian	High protector
Omar		Arabic	First born son
Omero		Italian	Known for his land holdings
Onslow		Anglo-Saxon	A hasty man's hill
Ora		Pacific Islands	Life
Orad		Australian	Earth
Oreste		Italian	Mountain man
Orin		Hebrew	Tree
Orion		Greek	The hunter. A constellation
Orlando	Orly	Italian, Spanish	Gives glory to his country

Name	Alternative spellings	Origin	Meaning
Orme		Anglo-Saxon	Kind
Oroiti		Pacific Islands	Slow-footed one
Oronzo		Italian	Swift, agile
Orran		Irish	Green-eyed
Orsen		Latin	Little bear
Orso		Italian	Bear
Ortensio		Italian	Gardener
Orvin	Orvyn	Anglo-Saxon	Brave friend
Osborne		Anglo-Saxon	Soldier of God
Osburt		Anglo-Saxon	Smart
Oscar		Italian	Warrior of God
Osgood		Anglo-Saxon	A good man
Osman		Arabic	A servant of God
Osmond		Anglo-Saxon	Divine protection
Oswald		Anglo-Saxon	Divine power
Othello		Spanish	Bold, title character of famous Shakespeare play
Otis		Greek	Keen of hearing
Otto		German	Wealthy
Ottone		Italian	Owner
Ovidio		Italian	Cattle owner
Owen		Welsh	Noble
Ox		American	Strong
Oz		Hebrew	Scholar, he who excels

P

Name	Alternative spellings	Origin	Meaning
Pablo		Spanish	Small. Name of famous artist Pablo Picasso
Paciano		Italian	Man of peace
Pacifico		Spanish	Man of peace
Paddy		Latin	Noble, well born
Paki		African	Witness
Pal		Scandinavian	Small
Palladin		Greek	Confrontational
Palmer		Anglo-Saxon	Open
Palmiro		Italian	Excellent
Pancho		Spanish	From France
Paolo		Italian, Spanish	Small
Par		Greek	God of the forest and shepherds
Paris		Greek	Mythical prince who fell in love with Helen of Troy
Parker		Anglo-Saxon	Park keeper
Pascal		Latin	Born at Easter
Pasha		Russian	Small
Pat		Latin	Noble, well born
Patrick		Latin	Noble, well born
Patton		Anglo-Saxon	Brash
Paul		Latin	Small
Pavel		Russian	Small
Pax		Latin	Peace
Paxton		Anglo-Saxon	From the warrior's estate
Pearson		Anglo-Saxon	Son of Piers
Pedro		Spanish	Rock
Pele		Hebrew	Miracle
Pepe		Spanish	God will add

Name	Alternative spellings	Origin	Meaning
Percival		French	He who pierces the valley. In legend, the knight who glimpsed the Holy Grail
Percy		French	He who pierces the valley
Peregrine		Latin	Stranger or pilgrim
Perry		American	Rock
Peter	Pete	Greek	Rock. One of Christ's disciples
Petya		Russian	Rock
Philip		Greek	Lover of horses
Philippe		French	Lover of horses
Philo		Greek	Loving, friendly
Phineas		Latin	An oracle
Phoenix		Greek	Legendary bird returns to life from ashes
Piero		Italian	Rock
Pierre		French	Rock
Piers		Greek	Rock
Pietro		Italian	Rock
Pindan		Australian	Desert
Pio		Italian	Pious, honest
Pip		Greek	From Phillip, lover of horses
Piper		Anglo-Saxon	Pipe or flute player
Piran		Cornish	Prayer. Patron Saint of Cornwall
Pitney		Scandinavian	Protector of the island
Placido		Italian, Latin	Calm, tranquil
Polaris		Latin	The North Star, used as a guide by navigators
Pollock		Anglo-Saxon	A fish. Surname of famous artist Jackson Pollock
Powys		Place name	Region in Wales

Name	Alternative spellings	Origin	Meaning
Prakash		Sanskrit	Light, or famous
Prasad		Sanskrit	Brightness
Prem		Sanskrit	Love
Presley		Anglo-Saxon	Priest's meadow
Preston		Anglo-Saxon	Priest's town
Primo		Latin	First
Prince		Latin	First in rank
Prospero		Italian	Happy, content, lucky

Q

Name	Alternative spellings	Origin	Meaning
Qabil		Arabic	Able
Qadir		Arabic	Powerful
Qasim	Quasim	Arabic	One who shares
Quentin		Latin	Fifth
Quigley		Scottish, Irish	One with messy hair
Quimby		Scandinavian	Estate of the woman
Quincy		Latin	Fifth
Quinlan		Scottish	Well built
Quinn		Irish	Fifth

R

Name	Alternative spellings	Origin	Meaning
Radko		Russian	Happy
Radley		Anglo-Saxon	Red meadow
Radosalve		Russian	Happy glory
Rafael		Spanish	God has healed
Rafferty		Irish, Scottish	Prosperous one
Rafi		Arabic	The exalted one
Rafiki		African	Friend
Rafiq		Arabic	Friend
Ragnar		Scandinavian	Military advisor
Rahman		Arabic	Merciful
Raimondo		Italian	Wise defender
Raj		Sanskrit	King
Rajendra		Sanskrit	A mighty king
Rajiv		Sanskrit	Striped
Ralph		Anglo-Saxon	Wolf counsellor
Ramesh		Sanskrit	Ruler of Rama
Ramiro		Italian, Spanish	Famous advisor
Ramon		Spanish	Wise defender
Ramsey		Anglo-Saxon	From the ram's island
Randolf	Randolph	Anglo-Saxon	Wolf shield
Randy		Anglo-Saxon	Wolf shield
Rangi		Pacific Islands	Heaven
Ranjit		Sanskrit	The delighted one
Raphael		Hebrew	God has healed
Rashad		African	Righteous
Rashid		Arabic	The well-guided one
Rasul		African	Messenger
Rata		Pacific Islands	A great chief
Rauf		Arabic	The compassionate one
Raul		Italian	Advisor, wolf

Name	Alternative spellings	Origin	Meaning
Raven		English	Large, black bird
Ravi		Sanskrit	Of the sun
Ray		French	The sovereign
Raymond		French	Wise defender
Reagan		Irish	Little king
Rebel		Latin	Rebellious one
Red		Anglo-Saxon	A primary colour
Redford		Anglo-Saxon	Red ford
Reece		Welsh	In love with life
Reeve		Anglo-Saxon	Steward
Regan		Irish	Little king
Regulus		Latin	The brightest star in the Leo constellation
Rehgan		Irish	Little king
Reid		Scottish	Red-head
Remington		Anglo-Saxon	English surname, from Rimington, in Yorkshire, meaning 'town on the boundary'
Remus		Latin	Fast. One of the brothers who founded Rome
Rémy		French	Oarsman
Renaldo		Spanish	Advisor to the king
Renato		Italian	Reborn
René		French	Reborn
Renoir		French	Name of famous artist, Pierre Auguste Renoir
Reuben	Ruben, Rubin	Hebrew	Behold a son
Rewan		Cornish	From St Rewan
Rex		Latin	A king
Rhett		Welsh	Keen

Name	Alternative spellings	Origin	Meaning
Rhodes		Place name	Greek island
Rhys		Welsh	Hero
Ricardo		Italian	Brave leader
Richard		Anglo-Saxon	Brave leader
Rico	Rick, Ricky	Spanish	Brave leader
Ridgley		Anglo-Saxon	From the ridge meadow
Riley		Irish	Brave
Rinaldo		Italian	Advisor to the king
Rio		Place name	Brazilian city
Ripley	Rypley	Anglo-Saxon	Lives in the noisy meadow
Ripper		American	Someone who tears
Ripple		Anglo-Saxon	Disturbance in smooth water
Roald		Scandinavian	Famous ruler
Roark	Roarke	Irish	Famous ruler
Roary		Irish	Fiery, red haired
Robert		Anglo-Saxon, German	Bright fame
Roberto		Italian	Bright fame
Robin	Robyn	Anglo-Saxon	Bright fame
Robson		Anglo-Saxon	Son of Robert
Rocco		Italian	Rest
Rochester		Anglo-Saxon	Camp on the rocks
Rock		Anglo-Saxon	Large stone
Rocky		Anglo-Saxon	Large stones
Roderick		Anglo-Saxon	Famous power
Roderigo		Spanish	Famous power
Rodolfo		Italian, Spanish	Famous wolf
Rodrigo		Italian, Spanish	Famous power
Rogelio		Spanish	Request
Roger		German	Famous spearman
Roland		Anglo-Saxon	Famous in the land
		German	Famous land
Rolando		Italian	Famous in the land

Name	Alternative spellings	Origin	Meaning
Rolf		German	Famous wolf
Roman		Anglo-Saxon	From Rome
Romano		Italian	From Rome
Romeo		Latin	Pilgrim to Rome. Name of Shakespeare's tragic lover in *Romeo and Juliet*
Romney		Welsh	Curving river
Romolo		Italian	Lives near a river
Ronald		Scottish	Rules with good judgement
Ronan		Irish	Little seal
Rongo		Pacific Islands	God of rain
Rooney		Scottish	The red one
Rorke		Irish	Famous ruler
Rory		German	Red ruler
Ross		Scottish	Lives on the headland
Rothwell		Scandinavian	From the red well
Rowan		Anglo-Saxon	A tree with berries
Roy		French	King
Royce		Anglo-Saxon	Son of the king
Royston		Anglo-Saxon	Town of Royce
Ruben	Reuben, Rubin	Hebrew	Behold a son
Rubeus		Greek	Red
Rudd		Anglo-Saxon	Ruddy complexion
Rudi		German	Famous wolf
Rudolf		German	Famous wolf
Ruel		Hebrew	Friend of God
Rufino		Italian	Red haired
Rufus		Latin	Red haired
Rune		Scandinavian	Secret lore
Rupert		German	Bright fame
Rurik		Russian	Famous power

Name	Alternative spellings	Origin	Meaning
Russell		Anglo-Saxon	Red haired
Rusty		Anglo-Saxon	From Russell, red haired
Rutledge		Anglo-Saxon	From the red pool
Ryan		Irish	Little king
Ryder		Celebrity child	(Kate Hudson)

S

Name	Alternative spellings	Origin	Meaning
Saad		African	Good fortune
Sabir		Arabic	The patient one
Sadik		Arabic	Truthful, or faithful
Saeed		African	Lucky
Saggitarius		Latin	The archer. Star sign and constellation
Said		African	Happy
Salaam		African	Peace
Salado		Spanish	Amusing
Salah		Arabic	Good, righteous
Salazar		Latin	Palace
Salim		Arabic	Safe
Salman		Arabic	Protector
Saloman		Hebrew	Peaceful
Salvador		Spanish	Saviour
Salvatore		Italian	Saviour
Salvo		Italian	Saviour
Sam		Hebrew	Asked of God
Sampson	Samson	Hebrew	Of the sun, or strong man
Samuel		Hebrew	Asked of God
Samuele		Italian	Asked of God
Sancho		Spanish	Saintly
Sanders		Anglo-Saxon	From Alexander, defender of mankind
Sandy	Sandie	Greek	Defender of mankind
Sanford		Anglo-Saxon	Negotiator
Sanjay		Sanskrit	Triumphant
Sankara		Sanskrit	Lucky
Sante		Italian	Saintly
Santiago		Spanish	St James
Santo		Italian	Saintly

Name	Alternative spellings	Origin	Meaning
Santos		Spanish	Saintly
Sarni		Arabic	The elevated one
Sasha		Russian	Defender of mankind
Satchel		Latin	Small bag
Saul		Hebrew	Asked for or prayed for
Saverio		Italian	Luminous
Saville		French	Stylish
Sawyer		Literary	*The Adventures of Tom Sawyer* by Mark Twain
Saxon		Anglo-Saxon	Germanic people
Sayed		Arabic	The lord, the master
Scanlan		Irish	Devious
Scorpio		Latin	Scorpion. Star sign and constellation
Scorpion		English	Scorpion, arachnid with a poisonous sting
Scott		Anglo-Saxon	From Scotland
Seamus		Irish	He who replaces
Sean	Shaun	Irish	God is gracious
Sebastian		Latin	From Bastia in Spain
Seff		Hebrew	A wolf
Seif		Arabic	Sword of religion
Selim		Arabic	Safe
Selwin	Selwyn	Anglo-Saxon	Friend at court
Senon		Spanish	Ivory treasure
Senwe		African	Dry grain stalk
Serafino		Italian	Shining angel
Serge		French	Servant
Sergei		Russian	Servant
Sergio		Italian	He who cares for
Seth		Hebrew	The appointed one, one of the sons of Adam in the Bible

Name	Alternative spellings	Origin	Meaning
Severo		Italian	Strict, severe
Severus		Latin	Strict, severe
Seville		Place name	Spanish city
Seyed		Arabic	The lord
Seymore		French	From town St Maur, in France
Shadow		English	Area of darkness
Shafiq		Arabic	Compassionate
Shaine		Irish	God is gracious
Shakar	Shakir	Arabic	Thankful
Shamrock		Anglo-Saxon	Plant, emblem of Ireland
Shamus		Irish	He who replaces
Shandy		Anglo-Saxon	Small and boisterous
Shane		Irish	God is gracious
Shankar		Sanskrit	He who gives happiness
Shannon		Irish	Old river
Sharif		Arabic	The honourable one
Sharma		Sanskrit	Protector
Shaun	Sean	Irish	God is gracious
Shauny		Irish	God is gracious
Shayne	Shane	Irish	God is gracious
Shelby		Anglo-Saxon	Willow farm
Sheldon		Anglo-Saxon	Farm on the ledge
Shelley		Anglo-Saxon	Farm on the ledge
Sher		Sanskrit	The beloved one
Sherlock		Literary	*The Adventures of Sherlock Holmes* by Sir Arthur Conan Doyle
Sherwin	Sherwyn	Anglo-Saxon	Quick as the wind
Shiloh		Hebrew	A place of rest
Shipley		Anglo-Saxon	From the sheep meadow
Shiva		Sanskrit	Benign. A Hindu god

Name	Alternative spellings	Origin	Meaning
Shmon		Hebrew	The listener
Shunnar		Arabic	Pleasant
Siddartha		Sanskrit	One who has accomplished his goal. A name of the Buddha
Sidney		French	A follower of St Denis
Siegfried		German	Peaceful victory
Siegmund		German	Victorious protector
Silas		Latin	Of the forest
Silvano		Italian	From the forest
Silvester	Sylvester	Latin	Of the forest
Silvestro		Italian	From the forest
Silvio		Italian	From the forest
Simon		Hebrew	The listener
Sinbad		Literary	*The Book of 1001 Arabian Nights*
Sinclair		Anglo-Saxon	St Clair
Sindri		Scandinavian	A mythical dwarf
Sinjon		Anglo-Saxon	St John
Sirio		Italian	The Dog Star
Sirius		Latin	The Dog Star, the brightest in the night sky
Skelly		Scottish	Historian
Skip		Scandinavian	Ship-owner
Slade		Anglo-Saxon	From the valley
Slater		American	From the surname
Smith	Smythe	Anglo-Saxon	Blacksmith
Smokey		Anglo-Saxon	Vapour from a fire
Sol		Latin	The sun
Solomon		Hebrew	Wise and peaceful
Sondre		Scandinavian	Uncertain
Soren		Scandinavian	Severe
Sorrel		French	Brown haired
Soul		English	Spirit
Sparky		American	Man about town

Name	Alternative spellings	Origin	Meaning
Sparrow		English	Small bird
Spike		English	Nickname for someone with spiky hair
Spirit		English	Soul, non-physical being
Stacey		Greek	Resurrection
Stanley		Anglo-Saxon	From the stoney meadow
Starr		Anglo-Saxon	Star
Stavros		Greek	Crowned
Stefan		German	Crown
Stefano		Italian	Crown
Stelios		Greek	Crown
Stéphane		French	Crown
Stephen	Steven, Steve, Stevie	Greek	Crown
Stewart	Stuart	Anglo-Saxon	Steward
Storm		Anglo-Saxon	Thunder and lightning
Sugar Ray		American	Name of famous boxer Sugar Ray Leonard
Sullivan		Irish	Dark eyes
Suman		Sanskrit	Cheerful and wise
Summit		English	Peak of a mountain
Sumner		Anglo-Saxon	Summoner
Suresh		Sanskrit	The ruler of the gods
Surya		Sanskrit	The sun
Sven		Scandinavian	Boy
Sverre		Scandinavian	Spinner, turner
Sweeney		Irish	Young hero
Symon		Hebrew	The listener

T

Name	Alternative spellings	Origin	Meaning
Tahir		African	Pure
Tahir		Arabic	Pure and virtuous
Taj		Sanskrit	Royal
Taji		African	Crown
Tajo		Spanish	Day
Talbot		French	Reward
Talib		African	Seeker
Taliesin		Welsh	Shining brow. Legendary Welsh poet
Tama		Pacific Islands	Son
Tamir		Arabic	Pure, tall
Tane		Pacific Islands	A Polynesian god
Tangaroa		Pacific Islands	Of the sea
Tariq		Arabic	The night visitor
Tarquin		Latin	Name of Roman kings
Tarun		Sanskrit	Young, tender
Tate		Anglo-Saxon	Uncertain
Taurus		Latin	The bull. Star sign and constellation
Tawhiri		Pacific Islands	A storm
Taylor		Anglo-Saxon	Cutter, clothes maker
Ted		Anglo-Saxon	From Edward, wealthy guardian
Terence		Latin	Tender, gracious
Terenzio		Italian	Soft, tender
Terry		Latin	Tender, gracious
Texas		Place name	US state
Thaddeus		Greek	Gift of God
Thane		Anglo-Saxon	Protective
Theo		Greek	God like

Name	Alternative spellings	Origin	Meaning
Theobald		Anglo-Saxon	Of the brave people
Théodore		French	Gift of God
Theodore		Greek	Gift of God
Théophile		French	Friend of God
Theron		Greek	A wild beast
Thierry		French	Ruler of the people
Thomas		Greek	A twin
Tiernan		Irish	Regal
Tiger		English	Striped predatory 'big' cat
Tiki		Pacific Islands	Spirit fetched from death to return to life
Timor		Place name	Island in Indonesia
Timothy	Tim	Greek	Honoured by God
Tipple		American	Slang for a drink
Titan		Greek	Giant
Tito		Italian	Defender
Titus		Greek	Giant
Tivon		Latin	Lover of nature
Tobias	Toby	Latin	God is good
Tobie	Toby	Latin	God is good
Todd		Latin	Fox
Tom	Thom	Greek	A twin
Tomas		Spanish	A twin
Tommaso		Italian	A twin
Tommy		Greek	A twin
Tomo		Greek	A twin
Tony	Toni	Latin	Praiseworthy
Tor		Anglo-Saxon	Rock formation on moorland peak
Tor	Thor	Scandinavian	From the god of thunder, Thor
Torrence		Latin	Smooth
Travis		Anglo-Saxon	Crossing

Name	Alternative spellings	Origin	Meaning
Trent		Latin	Quick-minded
Trevor		Irish	Prudent
Trey		American	Three in a suit of playing cards
Tristan	Trystan, Tristram	Welsh, Cornish	Sad. A tragic, romantic hero in Celtic legend
Tristram	Tristan, Trystan	Welsh	Sad. A tragic, romantic hero in Celtic legend
Troy		Irish	Foot soldier
Truman		Anglo-Saxon	Honest
Tucker		Anglo-Saxon	Garment maker, 'tucker of cloth'
Tuily		Irish	Interesting
Turi		Pacific Islands	A famous chief
Turner		Latin	Craftsman
Tyler		Anglo-Saxon	A tiler
Tyonne		American	Feisty
Tyrol		Place name	Region of the Alps
Tyrone		Irish	County in Northern Ireland
Tyson		French	High spirited

U

Name	Alternative spellings	Origin	Meaning
Ubora		African	Excellence
Udd		Hebrew	Praised
Ulan		African	First-born twin
Ulrich		German	Riches, power
Ulrik		Scandinavian	Powerful and wealthy
Ulysses		Greek	Angry one
Umar		Arabic, African	Long-lived
Umber		Anglo-Saxon	Orange, brown colour
Umberto		Italian	Magnificent giant
Unique		English	One of a kind
Urban		Latin	City dweller
Uriah		Hebrew	The light of God
Uriel		Hebrew	The light of God
Uriele		Italian	The light of God
Usher		Latin	Decisive
Ushnisha		Sanskrit	A crown
Usman		Arabic	A servant of God.
Utah		Place name	US state
Uther		Cornish	Legendary king, father of King Arthur
Utopia		Greek	Perfect place
Uwan		Australian	To meet

V

Name	Alternative spellings	Origin	Meaning
Vadim		Russian	To rule with greatness
Valentine		Latin	Strong, healthy; patron saint of lovers
Valentino		Italian	Strong, healthy; patron saint of lovers
Valerio		Italian	Courageous
Vamana		Sanskrit	Praiseworthy
Van		American	From Ivan or Evan, God is gracious
Vance		Anglo-Saxon	Brash
Vanya		Russian	Right
Varuna		Sanskrit	The God of the night sky
Vasili		Russian	King
Vassilly	Vassily	Russian	King
Vasudeva		Sanskrit	The father of the god Krishna
Vaughn		Welsh	Small
Vegas		Place name	From US city Las Vegas, the meadows
Vere		Anglo-Saxon	Alder tree
Vernon		Latin	Youthful
Victor	Vic	Latin	Conqueror
Vidal		Latin	Vital, lively
Vidya		Sanskrit	Knowledge
Vijay		Sanskrit	Strong and victorious
Viktor		Russian	Victory
Vimal		Sanskrit	Pure
Vince		Latin	Conqueror
Vincent		Latin	Conqueror
Vincenzo		Italian	Conqueror
Vinnie		Latin	Conqueror

Name	Alternative spellings	Origin	Meaning
Virgil		Latin	Strong
Vishnu		Sanskrit	The protector. A Hindu god
Vitale		Italian	Full of life
Vitali		Russian	Vitality
Vito		Italian	Belligerent
Vittore		Italian	Winner
Vittorio		Spanish	Winner
Vitya		Russian	Vitality
Vivian		French	Vivacious
Vlad		Russian	Ruler
Vladislav		Russian	Glorious rule
Vladja		Russian	Glorious rule
Vladmir		Russian	To rule with greatness
Voldemort		Latin	Flight from death
Volker		German	Prepared to defend
Volodya		Russian	To rule with greatness
Volya		Russian	To rule all

W

Name	Alternative spellings	Origin	Meaning
Wahib		Arabic	The generous one
Waitimu		African	Born of the spear
Waldo		German	Ruler
Walid		Arabic	The newborn boy
Wallace	Wallis	Anglo-Saxon	From Wales
Walter	Wally	Anglo-Saxon	Army ruler
Warra		Australian	Water
Warren		Anglo-Saxon	Watchman
Warwick		Place name	UK town
Wasim		Arabic	The handsome one
Wassily		Sanskrit	The God of the night sky
Wayne		Anglo-Saxon	Cart owner
Webster		Anglo-Saxon	Weaver
Wendel		German	Of the Wend people
Wilbur		Anglo-Saxon	Walled fort
Wilfred		Anglo-Saxon	Strong peacemaker
Wilhelm		German	Strong protector
Will		German	Strong protector
Willard		German	Courageous
William	Will	Anglo-Saxon	Strong protector
Willis		Anglo-Saxon	From William, strong protector
Wilson		Anglo-Saxon	Son of William
Windsor		Place name	UK town. Also the Royal family's surname
Winston		Anglo-Saxon	Friendly town. Also after Winston Churchill
Wolf		German	Wolf
Wolfgang		German	Wolf going

Name	Alternative spellings	Origin	Meaning
Woodrow		Anglo-Saxon	From the row of houses by the wood
Woody		Anglo-Saxon	Of the trees
Wordsworth		Anglo-Saxon	Surname of poet William Wordsworth
Worth		Anglo-Saxon	Enclosure
Wycliff		Anglo-Saxon	By the cliff
Wyndham		Anglo-Saxon	Hamlet near a path
Wynne		Anglo-Saxon	Friend

X

Name	Alternative spellings	Origin	Meaning
Xander		Greek	Defender of mankind
Xanthus		Greek	Golden haired
Xavier		French, Spanish, Italian	Luminous
Xen		American	From Zen
Xeno		Greek	Stranger
Xerxes		Arabic	Leader
Xyle		American	Helpful

Y

Name	Alternative spellings	Origin	Meaning
Yadon		American	Surname used as a first name
Yakim		Russian	Established by God
Yakov		Russian	He who replaces
Yale		Welsh	Arable upland
Yan		Hebrew	God's grace
Yancy		American	From Yankee
Yanis		Hebrew	God's grace
Yannis		Greek	Believer
Yardley		Anglo-Saxon	Fenced meadow
Yaroslav		Russian	Spring glory
Yarran		Australian	An acacia tree
Yasha		Russian	He who replaces
Yasir		Arabic	Wealthy
Yazid		Arabic	Ever increasing
Yeats		Literary	Surname of famous Irish poet W. B. Yeats
Yehudi		Hebrew	Praise to the Lord
Yoel		Hebrew	From Joel, Yaweh is God
Yohance		African	Gift from God
Yorick		Literary	*Hamlet* by William Shakespeare
York		Place name	UK city
Yukon		Place name	From US region meaning great river
Yuma		Place name	City in Arizona, USA
Yuri		Russian	Farmer
Yves		French	Yew

Z

Name	Alternative spellings	Origin	Meaning
Zaccheus		Hebrew	Unblemished
Zacharie		French	The Lord has remembered
Zachary	Zac	Hebrew	The Lord has remembered
Zachria		Hebrew	The Lord has remembered
Zade		Arabic	Flourishing
Zadok		Hebrew	Unyielding
Zafar		Arabic	The triumphant one
Zahir		African, Arabic	Shining
Zaie		American	Pleasure-seeking
Zain		American	Zany
Zaire		Place name	African country
Zakhar		Russian	God remembers
Zaki		Arabic	Pure
Zamir		Hebrew	A songbird
Zander		Greek	Defender of mankind
Zane		Literary	Name of writer Zane Grey
Zareb		African	Protector
Zavier		Spanish	Luminous
Zebediah		Hebrew	Gift of god
Zed		Hebrew	Energetic
Zekeriah		Hebrew	The Lord has remembered
Zen		Japanese	Spiritual
Zeth		Greek	Investigator
Zeus		Greek	The supreme god in Greek mythology
Zevi		Hebrew	Brisk
Zia		Arabic	Splendour or ripened grain
Zion		Hebrew	A sign
Zowie		Celebrity child	(David and Iman Bowie)
Zuri		African	Handsome

2

Girls' names
A to Z

A

Name	Alternative spellings	Origin	Meaning
Aaliyah		Arabic	Exalted
Aba		African	Born on Thursday
Abayomi		African	Come to bring joy
Abbie	Abby, Abbey	Hebrew	Father's joy
Abebi		African	Asked for
Abela		Italian	Breath
Abelia		Hebrew	Breath
Abelina		Italian	Breath
Abeo		African	Bringer of happiness
Abia		Arabic	Great
Abigail	Abby, Abi, Abbie	Hebrew	Father's joy
Abir		Arabic	Fragrant
Abla		African	Wild rose
Acacia		Greek	A flower/tree
Acorn		Anglo-Saxon	The seed of an oak tree
Ada		German	Noble
Adaeze		African	Princess

Name	Alternative spellings	Origin	Meaning
Adah		Hebrew	Adornment or ornament
Adalberta		German	Noble, famous
Adalgisa		German	Noble promise
Adalia		Hebrew	God is my refuge
Adan		Irish	Little fiery one
Adande		African	Challenger
Adanma		African	Daughter of beauty
Adanna		African	Father's daughter
Adanne		African	Mother's daughter
Adar		Arabic	Fire
Adara	Adhara	Arabic	Virgin. Name of a star
Addolorata		Italian	Sorrows
Adelaide		Italian	Noble
Adèle		French	Noble
Adelfina		Italian	Sisterly
Adelheide		German	Noble
Adelia		Italian	Noble
Adelinda		Italian	Noble
Adelpha		Greek	Sisterly
Adena		Hebrew	Delicate, slender
Adero		African	Life giver
Adiba		Arabic	Cultured
Adila		Arabic	Equal
Adiva		Arabic	Pleasant, gentle
Adjua		African	Born on Monday
Adoncia		Spanish	Owner
Adriana		Latin	From Hadria in Italy
Adrienne		French	From Hadria in Italy
Adwin		African	Artist
Adzo		African	Born on Monday
Aerien		French	Airy
Afam		African	Friendly
Afi		African	Born on Friday
Afraima		Arabic	Fruitful
Africa		Place name	A continent

Name	Alternative spellings	Origin	Meaning
Agafaya		Russian	Love
Agape		Greek	Love
Agatha		Greek	Kind, honourable
Agathe		French	Kind, honourable
Agbeko		African	Life
Aglaya		Russian	Beauty
Agnes		Greek	Pure, chaste
Agnessa		Russian	Chaste
Aidan		Irish	Little fiery one
Aidoo		African	Arrived
Aiesha		Arabic	Woman
Aileen		Scottish	Light bearer
Ailsa		Scottish	Island dweller
Aimée		French	Loved
Ain		Arabic	Precious
Aine		Irish	Grace
Aiofe		Irish	Beauty
Aisha		Arabic	Life
Aislin		Irish	Dream, vision
Aithne		Irish	Fire
Akala		Australian	A parrot
Akila		Arabic	Wise
Akilah		Arabic	Intelligent
Akili		African	Wisdom
Akilina		Russian	Eagle
Aksinya		Russian	Hospitality
Akuabia		African	Here is wealth
Akuako		African	Younger twin
Akwate		African	Older twin
Alaba		African	Second baby
Alaezi		African	Exonerated
Alana	Alannah	Irish	Attractive
Alanis	Alannis	Greek	From Atlanta, mythical city beneath the sea
Alatea		Spanish	Truth

Name	Alternative spellings	Origin	Meaning
Alayna		Irish	Attractive
Alberta		German	Noble and bright
Albertina		Italian	Noble and bright
Albina		Italian	White
Alda		Italian	Beautiful
Aldonza		Spanish	Sweet
Alea		French	Chance
Aleida		German	Noble
Alejandra		Spanish	Defender of mankind
Aleksandra		Russian	Defender of mankind
Aleksandrina		Russian	Defender of mankind
Alessandra		Greek	Defender of mankind
Alessandria		Greek	Defender of mankind
Alethea		Greek	Truth
Alex		Greek	Defender of mankind
Alexandra		Greek	Defender of mankind
Alexis		Greek	Defender of mankind
Alfonsina		Italian	Noble and brave
Alfreda		Italian	Counsellor of the elves
Alfredina		Italian	Counsellor of the elves
Ali		Arabic	Exalted
Alice		Greek	Wise, truthful one
Alicia	Alisha	Greek	Wise, truthful one
Alida		Latin	Small, winged one
Alima		Arabic	Musician, dancer
Alinga		Australian	The sun
Alison	Allie	Greek	Wise, truthful one
Alita	Alida	Spanish	Small, winged one
Aliya	Aliyah	Arabic	Sublime, exalted
Alize		French	Soft cloud
Alkina		Australian	The moon
Alkira		Australian	The sky
Allegra		Italian, Spanish	Joyful, lively
Alma		Hebrew	Of the soul

Name	Alternative spellings	Origin	Meaning
Almira		Arabic	Truth without question
Aloisia		Italian	In the light
Alvira	Elvira	Spanish	Foreign, stranger
Alvisa		Italian	Wise one of the household
Alyetoro		African	Peace on Earth
Alyona		Russian	Moon
Alyssa		Greek	Wise, truthful one
Alzena		Arabic	A woman
Ama		African	Born on Saturday
Amala		Arabic	Hope
Amalia		Italian	Energetic
Amalie		French	Hard working
Amana		Hebrew	Faithful or loyal
Amanda		Hebrew	Worthy of being loved
Amani		Arabic	Desire
Amara		Greek	Eternal beauty
Amarante		French	Flower
Amarina		Australian	Rain
Amaryllis		Greek	Shepherdess
Amata		Spanish	Beloved
Ambar		Sanskrit	Of the sky
Amber		Arabic	Golden orange gemstone
Ambra		Arabic	Golden orange gemstone
Ambretta		Italian	Golden orange gemstone
Ameerah	Amira	Arabic	Princess
Amélie		French	Hard working, industrious
Amerique		French	America
Amina		Arabic	Honest, faithful

Name	Alternative spellings	Origin	Meaning
Aminta		Greek	Protector
Amity		Latin	Friendship
Amrita		Sanskrit	Immortal
Anabelle		Latin	Loveable
Anaïs		French	Grace
Anan		Arabic	Of the clouds
Ananda		Sanskrit	Joyful
Anastasia		Russian	Resurrection
Anastasie		French	She who will rise again
Andrea		Greek	Strong
Andrée		French	Strong
Andy		Greek	Strong
Ange		French	Angel
Angel		English	Heavenly messenger
Angela		Greek	Heavenly messenger
Angelica		Greek	Heavenly messenger
Angelina		Italian	Angel
Angelou		Spanish	Angel
Anila		Sanskrit	Of the wind
Anisa		Arabic	Friendly
Anita		Italian	Grace
Anjanette		French	Blend of Anne and Janet
Anna		Italian	Grace
Anna Maria		Italian	Grace, bitter
Annabel		Italian	Grace, beauty
Annabella		Italian	Grace, beauty
Anne		Hebrew	Grace
Annika		Scandinavian	Gracious
Annisa		American	Blend of Anne and Lisa
Annissa		Arabic	Charming, gracious
Anouk		French	Grace
Anouska		Russian	Grace
Anthea		Hebrew	Flower like

Name	Alternative spellings	Origin	Meaning
Antoinette		French	Praiseworthy
Antonella		Italian	Praiseworthy
Antonia		Latin	Praiseworthy
Antonietta		Italian	Praiseworthy
Antonina		Russian	Praiseworthy
Anushka		Russian	Grace
Apanie		Australian	Water
Aphrodite		Greek	Goddess of beauty and love
Apple		Anglo-Saxon, celebrity child	A fruit (Gwyneth Paltrow and Chris Martin)
April		Latin	From first Roman month, start of spring
Aquarius		Latin	Water bearer. Star sign and constellation
Arabella		Latin	Beautiful altar
Araluen		Australian	The place of water lilies
Araminta		Greek	Fragrant flower
Aretha		Greek	The best
Aria		Latin	Beautiful melody
Ariana	Arianna	Latin	Most holy
Arianwyn		Welsh	Silver and fair, blessed
Arika		Australian	A water lily
Arina		Russian	Peace
Arinya		Australian	A kangaroo
Arlene		American, Scottish	Promise, pledge
Arlinda		American	Blend of Arleen and Linda
Artemisia		Italian	From Artemis, goddess of the moon and hunting
Aruna		Sanskrit	The dawn

Name	Alternative spellings	Origin	Meaning
Arwen		Literary	*The Lord of the Rings* by J. R. R. Tolkein
Arwyn		Welsh	Muse
Asa		Scandinavian	Divine
Ash		Anglo-Saxon	A tree
Asha		African, Sanskrit	Life Hope
Ashira		Hebrew	Wealthy
Ashley	Ashleigh	Anglo-Saxon	From the trees
Asia		Greek	East
Asta		Greek	A star
Astra		Greek	Like a star
Astrid		Scandinavian	Divine, beautiful
Asya		Russian	Resurrection
Athena		Greek	Goddess of wisdom and war
Atifa		Arabic	Affection
Atiya		Arabic	A gift
Atlanta		Place name	US city. From the mythical city beneath the waves
Audrey		Anglo-Saxon	Of noble strength
Aura		Greek	Of the air
Aurelia		Latin	Golden
Aurélie		French	Golden
Auretta		Italian	Gentle breeze
Auriga		Latin	Charioteer. A constellation
Aurora		Italian	Dawn, Roman goddess of the morning
Aurore		French	Dawn
Autumn		Anglo-Saxon	The season before winter
Ava		Greek	An eagle
Avalon		Celtic	An island paradise in Celtic mythology

Name	Alternative spellings	Origin	Meaning
Avara		Sanskrit	The youngest
Avril		French	April
Ayanna		African	Beautiful flower
Ayn		Russian	Grace
Azalea		Greek	A flower
Aziza		Arabic	Cherished one
Azra		Arabic	Virginal
Azure		English	Blue, green

B

Name	Alternative spellings	Origin	Meaning
Baako		African	First born
Baba		African	Born on Thursday
Babe		American	Slang for cute girl
Babette		French	Stranger
Badu		African	Tenth child
Bahati		African	Lucky
Bailey		French	Bailiff
Bakana		Australian	A watcher
Bala		Sanskrit	A young girl
Barakah		Arabic	Fair one
Barbara		Latin	Stranger
Barbro		Scandinavian	Stranger
Barina		Australian	The summit
Basimah		Arabic	The smiling one
Bathilda		Hebrew	Heroine
Bathsheba		Hebrew	Daughter of the oath
Batilda		Italian	Battler
Beatrice		Latin	Blessed, voyager through life
Beatrix		Anglo-Saxon	Bringer of happiness
Bega		Australian	Beautiful
Begonia		Latin	A flower
Belicia		Spanish	From Isabel, God's promise
Belinda		Italian	Beautiful, tender
Belita		Spanish	Little beauty
Bella		French	Beautiful
Bellatrix		Latin	Female warrior
Belle		French	Beautiful

Name	Alternative spellings	Origin	Meaning
Belphoebe		Literary	*The Faeirie Queen* by Edmund Spenser
Benada		African	Born on Tuesday
Benedicta		Latin	Blessed
Bennath		Cornish	Blessing
Berenice		Greek	Bringer of victory
Bernadette		French	Brave as a bear
Berry		Anglo-Saxon	Like a fruit
Berta		German	Bright, famous
Bertha		German	Bright, famous
Beryl		Greek	Precious green gem
Beth		Hebrew	My God is a vow
Bethany		Hebrew	House of figs
Betty		Hebrew	From Elizabeth, God is my vow
Beyonce		American	From the Creole surname Beyince
Bianca		Italian	White
Bibi		Arabic	A lady
Bibiana		Italian	Lively
Bijou		French	Jewel
Billie		Anglo-Saxon	Strong protector
Binah		African	Dancer
Binda		Australian	Deep water
Binta		African	With God
Birgit		Scandinavian	Exalted one
Bisa		African	Loved
Blaine		Irish	Slender
Blejan		Cornish	Bloom
Bliss		English	Happiness
Blodeyn		Welsh	Flower
Blodwedd		Welsh	In Celtic legend, a bride of flowers

Name	Alternative spellings	Origin	Meaning
Blossom		Anglo-Saxon	Flowers on fruit trees
Bluebell		Anglo-Saxon	A blue woodland flower
Blythe		Anglo-Saxon	Cheerful
Bobby		Anglo-Saxon	Bright fame
Bogdana		Russian	Gift from God
Bonita		Spanish	Pretty
Bonnie		Anglo-Saxon	Pretty
Bonte		French	Bounty
Borra		Cornish	Dawn
Bracha		Hebrew	A blessing
Bramble		Anglo-Saxon	Prickly plant
Brangwen	Branwen	Welsh	Fair, blessed
Breeze		English	A light wind
Bridget	Brighid, Brigid	Irish	The exalted one. Celtic goddess of light and poetry
Brie	Bree	French	Marshland
Brier		French	Heather
Brigida		Italian	Exalted one
Brigitte		French	The exalted one
Britt		Scandinavian	Exalted one
Brittany		Latin	From Britain
Bronagh		Welsh	Sorrowful
Bronnen		Cornish	A rush
Brontë		Literary	From the surname of authors Emily and Charlotte Brontë
Bronwen		Welsh	Fair, blessed
Bronze		English	Precious metal
Brook	Brooke	Anglo-Saxon	A small stream
Bruna		Italian	Brown
Bryluen		Cornish	Rose

Name	Alternative spellings	Origin	Meaning
Bryn		Welsh	A hill
Bryony		Greek	A vine
Buena		Spanish	Good one
Bunme		African	My gift

C

Name	Alternative spellings	Origin	Meaning
Cairo		Place name	Capital of Egypt
Caitlin		Irish	Pure
Cal		Welsh	Dove
Cala		Arabic	Fortress
Calico		American	Cotton fabric
Calla		Greek	Beautiful
Callidora		Greek	Beautiful gift
Callista		Greek	Most beautiful one
Calypso		Greek	Mythical nymph who fell in love
Camden		Place name	Area in North London
Camelia		Latin	A flower
Camilla		Latin	Noble
Camille		Latin	Virginal, unblemished
Camira		Australian	Of the wind
Candice	Candace, Candy	Latin	Brilliance, clarity
Candida		Italian	Bright white
Cantara		Arabic	Bridge
Caoimhe		Irish	Gentle, beauty, grace
Capri		Place name	Italian island
Capucine		French	Cowl
Caresse		French	Beloved
Carezza		Italian	Caress
Carina	Karina	Latin	Ship's keel. A constellation
Carissa		Latin	Most beloved one
Carla		Italian	Strong
Carlotta		Italian	Free
Carmel		Hebrew, Latin	Garden, orchard

Name	Alternative spellings	Origin	Meaning
Carmela		Italian	Divine garden
Carmelita		Spanish	Divine garden
Carmen		Spanish	Garden
Carmilla		Hebrew	Garden, orchard
Carnation		English	Flower
Carola		Italian	Strong
Carole		Anglo-Saxon	Strong
Carolina		Italian	Strong
Carolyn		English	Womanly
Caron		French, Welsh	Pure / To love
Carroll		Literary	From the author Lewis Carroll
Carwyn		Welsh	Blessed, fair love
Cary		Welsh	Descendant of the dark ones
Carys		Welsh	Love
Casey		Irish	Brave
Cassandra		Greek	Trojan princess who could foresee disaster
Cassia		Latin	From the cassia (cinnamon) tree
Catalina		Spanish	Pure
Catena		Italian	Pure
Caterina		Italian	Pure
Catherine		Greek	Pure
Cayla		American	From Kayleigh, slender
Cécile		French	Blind one
Cecilia		Latin	Blind one
Celena	Celina	Greek	Goddess of the moon
Celene	Celine	Greek	Goddess of the moon
Celeste		Latin	Heavenly

Name	Alternative spellings	Origin	Meaning
Celyn		Welsh	Holly
Ceri		Welsh	Blessed, fair poet, goddess of poetic inspiration
Ceridwen		Welsh	Blessed, fair poet, goddess of poetic inspiration
Cerise			Dark, bright pink
Cerulean		English	A shade of deep blue
Cerys		Welsh	Love
Cesarina		Italian	Hairy
Cézanne		French	Surname of artist, Paul Cézanne
Chai		Hebrew	Life giving
Chanah		Hebrew	Grace
Chandani		Sanskrit	The goddess Devi
Chandi		Sanskrit	Name of goddess Sakti
Chandra		Sanskrit	Bright moon
Chanel	Chanelle	French	Pipe, channel. Name of French designer, Coco Chanel
Chantal		French	Song
Chante		French	To sing
Charis		Greek	Grace, charm
Charisma		Greek	Charm and grace
Charissa		Greek	Grace, charm
Charity		Latin	Loving and generous
Charlene		French	Small beauty
Charlize		French	Free
Charlotte		French	Small and pretty
Charmaine		Latin	Charming
Chartreuse		French	A French liqueur, a shade of green
Chastity		Latin	Pure and chaste

Name	Alternative spellings	Origin	Meaning
Chaton		French	Kitten
Chaya		Hebrew	Life
Chelsea		Anglo-Saxon	Landing place
Cherry		English	Fruit
Cheryl		French	Dear
Chiara		Italian	Clear, illustrious
Chiku		African	Talkative
China		Place name	Country
Chinue		African	Blessing
Chiquita		Spanish	Little one
Chloe		Greek	Fertile young woman
Cho		Chinese	Beautiful
Chocolate		English	Food and colour
Chorus		English	Refrain in a song, or a choir of voices
Chris		Latin	Follower of Christ
Christa		German	Follower of Christ
Christelle		French	Follower of Christ
Christer		Scandinavian	Follower of Christ
Christiane		French	Follower of Christ
Christina		Latin	Follower of Christ
Christine		French	Follower of Christ
Chrysilla		Greek	Golden haired
Ciara		Italian, Welsh	Clear, illustrious / Little dark one
Cilla		Greek	From Lucilla, light
Cindy		Greek	From Lucinda, light
Cinzia		Italian	Moon
Circe		Greek	Witch in Greek mythology
Cirilla		Italian	Queen
Cirrus		Anglo-Saxon	A form of cloud
Claire	Clare	Latin	Clear, illustrious
Clara		Italian	Clear, shining
Clarice		Latin	Little brilliant one

Name	Alternative spellings	Origin	Meaning
Clarissa		Latin	Intelligent, clear thinking
Claudette		French	Lame one
Claudia		Latin	Lame one
Claudine		French	Lame one
Clémence		French	Compassionate
Cleo	Clio	Greek	Glorious one
Cloud		Anglo-Saxon	Water vapour in the sky
Clover		Anglo-Saxon	Clover
Cochiti		Spanish	Forgotten
Coco		Spanish	From the cocoa plant, ingredient of chocolate
Cody		American	Helpful
Colette		French	Victory of the people
Colleen		Irish	Young girl
Connie		Latin	From Constance
Consuelo		Spanish	Consolation
Cookie		American	Cute
Coorah		Australian	Woman
Cora		American, Greek	Judgement Maiden
Coral		Latin	From the sea
Corazon		Spanish	Heart
Coretta		Literary	From Cora, maiden, invented for *The Last of the Mohicans* by James Fenimore Cooper
Corey		Irish	Ravine
Corinna		Italian	Young girl
Corinne		French	Young girl
Cornelia		Latin	A horn
Coro		Italian	Chorus

Name	Alternative spellings	Origin	Meaning
Cortesia		Spanish	Hill
Cosima		Greek	Perfect harmony
Courtney		French	Courteous
Crimson		English	A shade of red
Crisanta		Latin	From the flower chrysanthemum
Crispina		Italian	Curly haired
Cristiano		Italian	Follower of Christ
Cristina		Italian	Follower of Christ
Crystal		Anglo-Saxon, Greek	Beautiful rock form Clear as ice
Crystin		Welsh	Christian
Cyan		English	Pale blue
Cybill	Cybil, Sybill	Latin	Prophet
Cygnus		Latin	Swan, a constellation
Cynthia		Greek	Moon goddess

D

Name	Alternative spellings	Origin	Meaning
Dagmar		Scandinavian	Dear, peaceful girl
Dagna	Dag, Dagne	Scandinavian	New day
Dahlia		Latin	A flower
Daisy		Anglo-Saxon	Eye of the day
Dakota		American	American place name, Native American tribe
Dalia	Dahlia	Italian	After the flower dahlia
Dalila		Italian	From Delilah, poor
Damara		Greek	Gentle girl
Damask		English	Grey, pink
Damiana		Italian	Tamer
Damisi		African	Happy
Dana		Irish	God is my judge
Dandelion		Anglo-Saxon	A bright yellow flower
Daniela		Italian	God is my judge
Danielle		French	God is my judge
Dante		Latin	Enduring. Name of poet Dante Alighieri, author of *The Divine Comedy*
Danza		Italian	Dancer
Daphne		Greek	Nymph who turned into a laurel tree
Dara		Hebrew	Compassionate
Darcy		Anglo-Saxon	Valley town
Daria		Greek	Wealthy
Darlene		French	Darling
Darri		Australian	A track
Davina		Hebrew	The beloved one
Dawn		Anglo-Saxon	Daybreak

Name	Alternative spellings	Origin	Meaning
Daya		Hebrew	Bird
Dayla		Anglo-Saxon	Valley
Daytona		Place name	US city
Deandra		American	Blend of Deirdre and Alexandra
Deborah		Hebrew	The bee (worker)
Deianeira		Greek	Wife of Hercules
Deirdre		Irish	Tragic Irish heroine
Deja		French	Before
Delfina		Italian	Dolphin
Delia		Greek	Name for goddess of the moon and hunting
Delice		French	Delight
Delilah		Hebrew	Beautiful temptress
Delinda		Italian	Anointed
Dell		Greek	Kind
Della	Adela	German	Noble
Dellen		Cornish	Petal
Delma		Spanish	Beauty, eternal goodness
Delores		Spanish	Sorrowful
Delphine		Latin	Woman from Delphi, or from the flower delphinium
Delphinium		Latin	A tall flower
Delwyn		Welsh	Pretty, blessed
Demelza		Cornish	Cornish place name. Heroine of Winston Graham's Poldark novels
Demetria		Italian	From Demeter, Greek goddess of agriculture
Demi		Latin	Half
Deneb		Arabic	Tail. Name of a star

Name	Alternative spellings	Origin	Meaning
Denise		Greek	Wine lover
Dervla		Irish	Daughter of Ireland
Desiree		French	Desire
Destiny		English	Fate
Devika		Sanskrit	A little goddess
Devon	Devona	Place name	English county
Dewi		American	Fresh
Deyanira		Greek	Devastating
Dharma		Sanskrit	Morality
Diamanta		French	Like diamonds
Diana		Latin	Divine. Goddess of hunting and the moon
Diane	Dian	French	Divine
Dido		Greek	Name of a queen
Dietlind		German	Tender people
Dilwen		Welsh	True, genuine and blessed
Dilys		Welsh	Genuine, steadfast
Dina		Italian	Judgement
Dinah		Latin	Judgement
Dione	Dionne	Greek	Wine lover
Dior		French	From fashion designer Christian Dior
Disa		Scandinavian	Divine
Diva		English	Renowned singer
Divine		English	God like
Doherty		Irish	Obstructive
Doli		African	Doll
Dolly		American	Doll
Dolores		Spanish	Lady of sorrows
Domenica		Italian	Belongs to God
Dominga		Spanish	Belongs to God
Dominique		French	Belongs to God
Donatella		Italian	Donated to God

Name	Alternative spellings	Origin	Meaning
Dora		Greek	A gift
Dore		French	Golden
Doreen		French	Golden
Dori		French	Golden
Dorian		Greek	Happy
Doris		Greek	Greek goddess of the sea
Dorota		Spanish	God's gift
Dorotea		Italian	God's gift
Dorothée		French	Gift of God
Dorothy		Greek	Gift of God
Dove		English	Bird, symbol of peace
Dream		English	Vision
Drew		Greek	Strong
Drina		Spanish	From Hadria in Italy
Drusilla		Latin	Strong
Duena		Spanish	Protect the companion
Dulcie		Latin	Sweet
Dulcinea		Literary	*Don Quixote* by Miguel de Cervantes
Duna		Italian	Sand dune
Durga		Sanskrit	Unattainable. A Hindu goddess
Dusk		Anglo-Saxon	End of the day
Dusty		American	Name of singer Dusty Springfield

E

Name	Alternative spellings	Origin	Meaning
Eartha		Anglo-Saxon	Earthy
Ebba		German	Boar
Ebony		Greek	Black wood
Ebrel		Cornish	April
Echo		Greek	Name of a nymph in Greek mythology
Ecstasy		English	Bliss
Edda		German	Uncertain
Eden		Hebrew	Pleasure, place of pleasure
Edith		Anglo-Saxon	Prosperous in war
Edna		Hebrew	Pleasure
Edwina		Anglo-Saxon	Prosperous friend
Effie		Greek	Virtuous
Efia		African	Born on Friday
Egypt		Place name	African country
Eileen		Irish	Light bearer
Eira		Welsh	Snow
Ekala		Australian	A lake
Elaine		Greek	Light of the sun
Elda		Italian	Gift of the sun
Eldora		Spanish	Gift of the sun
Eleanor		Greek	Light of the sun
Electra	Elektra	Greek	Brilliant, shining
Elegy		American	Tribute
Elena		Italian	Light of the sun
Eleonora		Italian	Light of the sun
Eletta		Italian	Elite
Eliana		Italian	Yaweh is my God
Elisa		Italian	Yaweh is my God
Elisabetta		Italian	God is my vow

Name	Alternative spellings	Origin	Meaning
Élise		French	God is my vow
Elisha		Hebrew	God is my salvation
Elissa		Hebrew	Consecrated to God
Eliza		Hebrew	Consecreated to God
Elizabeth		Hebrew	Consecrated to God
Elke		German	Noble
Ella		Italian	Light of the sun
Elle		French	Woman
Ellie		Greek	Light of the sun
Ellin		Australian	To move
Elma		Arabic	Sweet
Elodie		French	Wealthy
Élodie		French	Wealthy stranger
Eloise		French	Intelligent
Elsa		German	God is my vow
Else		Hebrew	Consecrated to God
Elspeth		Scottish	God is my oath
Elvia		Italian	Elfin
Elvina		Anglo-Saxon	Elfin
Elvira		Spanish	Truly foreign
Elwyn		Anglo-Saxon	Elf/wise friend
Elysia		Greek	From the blessed isles
Ema		Pacific Islands	Beloved
Emanuela		Italian, Hebrew	God is with us
Ember		American	Variation of Amber
Emerald		Anglo-Saxon	Precious green gem
Emil		German	Rival
Emilia		Italian	Rival

Name	Alternative spellings	Origin	Meaning
Émilie		French	Rival
Emily		German	Poised
Emma		German	Whole, universal
Emmanuel	Emmanuella	Hebrew	God is with us
Emmanuelle		French	God is with us
Emmeline		German	Work
Ena		Irish	Fire
Engracia		Spanish	Graceful
Enid		Welsh	Lively
Enor		Cornish	Honour
Enrica		Italian,	Ruler of the Spanish home
Eowyn		Literary	*The Lord of the Rings* by J. R. R. Tolkein
Eponin		Literary	*Les Misérables* by Victor Hugo
Erika		Scandinavian	Honourable
Erin		Irish	From Ireland
Erma		Latin	Wealthy
Ermentrude		German	Whole, strong
Ernestina		Italian	Brave like an eagle
Eshe		African	Life
Esmeralda		Spanish	Emerald
Esperanza		Spanish	Hope
Estelle		Latin	A star
Ester		Spanish	Like a star
Esther		Arabic	A star
Etenia		American	Native American word for riches
Ethel		Anglo-Saxon	Noble
Etta		Anglo-Saxon	From Henrietta, ruler of the home
Eudora		Greek	Good gift
Eunice		Greek	Victorious

Name	Alternative spellings	Origin	Meaning
Euphoria		English	Extreme happiness
Eustacia		Greek	Fruitful
Eva		Italian	Life giving
Evangelia		Greek	One who brings good news
Eve		Hebrew	Life giving
Evelyn		Hebrew	Life giving
Ezra		Hebrew	Happy

F

Name	Alternative spellings	Origin	Meaning
Fabiana		Italian	Bean grower
Fabiola		Italian	Bean grower
Fabrizia		Italian	Craftsman
Fadhila		African	Outstanding
Fadila		Arabic	Generous and distinguished
Faith		English	Belief
Faiza		Arabic	Victorious
Farah		Arabic	Happiness
Farida		Arabic	Unique
Fatima		Arabic	Daughter of the prophet Mohammed
Fatin		Arabic	Captivating
Fausta		Italian	Lucky
Fawn		English	Young deer
Fay	Faye	Anglo-Saxon	Fairy
Federica		Italian	Brave peacemaker
Fedora		Russian	Gift of God
Fedra		Italian	Brave peacemaker
Felicia		Latin	Happy
Felicita		Italian	Lucky one
Felicity		Latin	Lucky, fortunate
Felipa		Spanish	Lover of horses
Felita		Latin	Happy
Fen		Anglo-Saxon	Flat coastal plain
Ferdinanda		Italian	Brave peacemaker
Fern		Anglo-Saxon	A plant
Ffion		Welsh	Fair
Fiamma		Italian	Flame
Fidelia		Spanish	Faithful one
Fiero		Italian	Proud
Fifi		French	From Josephine, God will add

Name	Alternative spellings	Origin	Meaning
Filiberta		Italian	Bright, shining
Filippa		Italian	Lover of horses
Fiona		Welsh	Fair
Fiore		Italian	Flower
Fiorenze		Italian	Flourishing
Fioretta		Italian	Flourishing
Flamingo		English	Beautiful pink bird
Flavia		Italian	Golden
Fleur		Latin	Flower
Fleurette		French	Little flower
Flora		Latin	Flower
Florence		Latin, place name	Blossoming Italian city
Florida		Latin	Floral
Flower		English	Plant blossom
Fortuna		Latin	Fate
Fosca		Italian	Dark
Fossetta		French	Dimpled
Franca		Italian	From France
Frances		Latin	Free woman/from France
Francesca		Italian	From France
Francine		Italian	From France
Francisca		Spanish	From France
Françoise		French	From France
Frankie		Latin	Free woman/from France
Frédérique		French	Brave peacemaker
Freja	Freya, Freia	Scandinavian	Lady, goddess of love
Frida		Italian	She who has found peace
Frieda	Friede	German	Peace
Fuschia		Latin	Flowering shrub

G

Name	Alternative spellings	Origin	Meaning
Gabriel		Hebrew	God is my strength, name of an archangel
Gabriella		Italian	God is my strength
Gabrielle		French	God is my strength
Gaea	Gaia	Greek	Earth goddess
Gail		Hebrew	Father's joy
Gala		Russian	Calm
Galadriel		Literary	*The Lord of the the Rings* by J. R. R. Tolkein
Galaxia		Spanish	Galaxy
Galia		Hebrew	God has redeemed
Galina	Galena	Russian	Calm
Galya		Russian	Calm
Gardenia		Latin	A flower
Garland		French	Chain of blossoms
Gay		French	Happy
Gayle		Hebrew	Father's joy
Gazelle		Latin	Antelope
Gedala		Australian	The day
Geena		American	From the farm
Gemella		Italian	Twin sister
Gemini		Latin	Twins, star sign and constellation
Gemma		Latin	Precious stone
Geneva		French	Junier tree
Geneviève		French	Fair, blessed, soft
Georgia		Greek	From the farm
Georgina	Georgia	Greek	Girl from the farm
Geraldina		Italian	Precious stone
Gerd	Gerda	Scandinavian	Norse goddess of fertility

Name	Alternative spellings	Origin	Meaning
Germaine		French	From Germany
Gertrude	Gertrud	German	Strong, spear
Ghada		Arabic	Graceful
Ghalyela		African	Precious
Ghera		Australian	A gum leaf
Giada		Italian	Jade
Gianna		Italian	God is gracious
Gilda		Italian, German	Sacrifice Gilded
Gillian	Gill, Gillie	Latin	Youthful
Gimbya		African	Princess
Gina		Greek, Italian	Girl from the farm God is gracious
Ginevra		Italian	Fair, blessed, smooth, soft
Ginny		Latin	From Virginia, chaste, pure, or Ginevra, fair, blessed, smooth, soft
Giorgia		Italian	From the farm
Giovanna		Italian	God is gracious
Giselda		Italian	Heroine
Giselle	Gisella	Italian	Heroine
Gita		Sanskrit	A song
Gitana		Spanish	Gypsy
Gladys		Welsh	Country
Glen		Scottish	Secluded valley
Glenda		Welsh	Pure, holy
Glenys		Welsh	Pure, holy
Gloria		Latin	Glorious
Glynis		Welsh	Pure, holy
Godiva		Anglo-Saxon	Gift from God
Goldie		Anglo-Saxon	From gold, precious metal
Grace		Latin	Graceful

Name	Alternative spellings	Origin	Meaning
Grainne		Irish	From 'grain'. Daughter of an Irish king
Granya		Irish	From 'grain'. Daughter of an Irish king
Grazia		Italian	Grace
Graziella		Italian	Grace
Greer		Greek	Watchful mother
Greta		Italian	Pearl
Gudrun		Scandinavian	Divine, secret lore
Guendalina		Italian	Blessed ring
Guinevere	Gweniver	Welsh, Cornish	Fair, blessed, smooth, soft. Legendary wife of King Arthur
Gulara		Australian	Moonlight
Gwaynten		Cornish	Spring
Gwen		Welsh	Fair, blessed
Gwendolin		Welsh	Blessed ring
Gweneth		Welsh	A region of Wales
Gwiryon		Cornish	Sincere
Gwyn		Welsh	Fair, blessed
Gwynder		Cornish	Brightness
Gwynedd		Welsh	A region of Wales
Gwyneth		Welsh	A region of Wales
Gyneth		Literary	*The Bridal of Triermain* by Sir Walter Scott

H

Name	Alternative spellings	Origin	Meaning
Habiba		Arabic	Beloved
Hadya		Arabic	A leader or guide
Haiba		African	Charm
Haifa		Arabic	Slender
Hali		Greek	Sea
Halla		African	Unexpected gift
Halle		Anglo-Saxon	Heroine
Hamida		African	Gracious
Hana		Arabic	Bliss, happiness
Hanna		African	Happiness
Hannah		Hebrew	Favoured by God, or graceful
Hanya		Australian	A stork
Harmony		Greek	In accord
Harper		English	Harp player
Harriette		French	Ruler of the home
Hasna		Arabic	Beautiful
Hava		Hebrew	Lovely
Havana		Place name	Capital of Cuba
Hawlee		American	From Hayley, from the hay meadow
Hayfa		Arabic	Slender
Hayley		Anglo-Saxon	From the hay meadow
Hazel		Anglo-Saxon	Hazel tree
Heather		Anglo-Saxon	Small heathland flower
Heaven		English	
Hedia		Hebrew	Voice of the Lord
Hedwig	Hedda	German	Contentious war
Heidi		German	Noble
Helen		Greek	Light/reed
Hélène		French	Light of the sun

Name	Alternative spellings	Origin	Meaning
Helga		Anglo-Saxon, Scandinavian	Blessed, prosperous
Helima		Arabic	Kind, gentle
Henriette		French	Ruler of the home
Hermione		Greek	Handsome one, earthy
Hermosa		Spanish	Beautiful
Hertha		Scandinavian	Norse goddess of fertility
Hester		Greek	Star
Hika		Pacific Islands	Daughter
Hilary		Latin	Cheerful one
Hilda	Hilde	German	Battle
Hiriwa		Pacific Islands	Silver
Hoku		Pacific Islands	A star
Holly		Anglo-Saxon	Holly tree
Honey		English	Sweet food produced by bees
Honour		Latin	Honourable one
Hope		English	Feeling that something desired may happen
Hortense		French	Garden
Hulda		Scandinavian	Sweet, lovable
Hyacinth		Latin	A flower
Hypatia		Greek	Intellectual

I

Name	Alternative spellings	Origin	Meaning
Ianthe		Greek	Flower
Ida		Italian	Island where Zeus was born
Idril		Literary	*The Silmarillion* by J. R. R. Tolkein
Ikea		Scandinavian	Smooth
Ileana		Italian	Trojan
Ilse		German	God is my vow
Imam		Arabic	One who believes in God
Iman		Arabic	Believer
Imelda		Italian, Spanish	Light of the sun
Imena		African	Dream
Imogen		Latin	Like her mother
Ina		Irish	Fire
Inas		Pacific Islands	Wife of the moon
India		Place name	Asian country
Indiana		Place name	US state
Indigo		Greek	Deep blue
Indira		Sanskrit	An alternative name for the wife of the god Vishnu
Ines		Italian	Chaste
Inès		French	Chaste
Infinity		English	Eternity, endlessness
Ingrid	Inger	Scandinavian	From the Norse fertility god, beautiful
Innocence		English	Without crime or guile
Iola		Greek	Dawn
Iolanthe		Greek	Flower
Ira		Hebrew	Contented
Ireland		Celebrity child	(Alec Baldwin and Kim Basinger)

Name	Alternative spellings	Origin	Meaning
Ireland		Place name	Country
Irene		Greek	Peace
Irina		Russian	Peace
Iris		Greek	Goddess of the rainbow
Irma		Latin	Strong woman
Irmina		Italian	Strong woman
Isa		Scottish	Luminous
Isabel		Spanish	Consecrated to God
Isabella		Italian	Consecrated to God
Isabelle		French	Consecrated to God
Isadora		Greek, Italian	Gift of the goddess Isis
Isla		Scottish	From the Hebridean island Islay
Isleta		Spanish	Island
Isotta		Italian	Protects with fire
Isra		Arabic	Journeying by night
Israt		Arabic	Affection
Iva		Italian	God is gracious
Ivana		Russian	God is gracious
Ivory		English	Pale cream, material of elephant tusks
Ivy		Anglo-Saxon	Plant name
Izzy		American	From Isadora, gift of the goddess Isis

J

Name	Alternative spellings	Origin	Meaning
Jacaranda		Greek	A flower
Jacey		American	Form of jacinda (a flower)
Jacinda		Greek	A flower
Jackie		Hebrew	The one who replaces
Jacqueline	Jaqualine	French	The supplanter
Jacquetta	Jacquette	French	The supplanter
Jada		Anglo-Saxon	Semi-precious green gem
Jade		Anglo-Saxon	Semi-precious green gem
Jadelyn		American	Blend of Jade and Lynne
Jaela	Jael	Hebrew	Mountain goat
Jaime	Jamee	Hebrew	The one who replaces
Jaira		Spanish	Jehova teaches
Jala		Arabic	Clarity
Jalia		African	Prominent
Jalila	Jalilah	Arabic	Great
Jalini		Sanskrit	Lives next to the ocean
Jama		Sanskrit	Daughter
Jamaica		Place name	Caribbean island
Jamais		French	Never
Jamal		Arabic	Beautiful one
Jamelia		Arabic	Beautiful
Jamila	Jamilah	Arabic	Beautiful
Jana		Russian	God is gracious
Janan		Arabic	Heart, soul
Jane		Hebrew	God is gracious
Janelle		French	God is gracious

Name	Alternative spellings	Origin	Meaning
Janessa		Literary	A mix of Jane and Vanessa, invented for *Guilliver's Travels* by Jonathan Swift
Janet		Scottish	God is gracious
Janice		Hebrew	God is gracious
Janna		Arabic	Fruit harvest
Jannali		Australian	The moon
Jarita		Sanskrit	A legendary bird
Jarnila		Arabic	Beautiful
Jarrah		Australian	A type of tree
Jasmine		Arabic	A small fragrant white flower
Jaxine		American	Form of jacinda (a flower)
Jay		American	Jaybird
Jaya		Sanskrit	Victory
Jayden	Jaydon	Hebrew	Thankful
Jean	Jeanne	French	God is gracious
Jeannine		French	God is gracious
Jehan		Arabic	Beautiful flower
Jemima		Hebrew	A dove
Jenna		Cornish	God is Gracious
Jennifer	Jenny	Welsh	Fair, blessed, smooth, soft
Jensine		Scandinavian	God is gracious
Jeri		American	Appointed by God
Jessalyn		American	Blend of Jessica and Lynn
Jesse		Hebrew	God's gift
Jessica		Hebrew	Wealthy
Jewel		English	Precious gem
Jezebel		Hebrew	Impure
Jiba		Australian	The moon

Name	Alternative spellings	Origin	Meaning
Jillian	Jill, Gill	Latin	Youthful
Jira		Arabic	Blood relative
Jirra		Australian	A kangaroo
Joan		Anglo-Saxon	God is gracious
Joanne	Jo, Joanna	Hebrew	God is gracious
Jocelyn		American	Blend of Joyce and Lynn
Jodie		Hebrew	Woman from Judea
Joelle		Hebrew	The Lord is God
Jolan		Hungarian	Violet
Jolene		Hebrew	God will add
Jolie		French	Happy
Joplin		American	From surname of rock star Janis Joplin
Joquil		Latin	A flower
Jora		Hebrew	Autumn rain
Jordan	Jordana, Jordane	Hebrew	Flowing down (as in the River Jordan)
Josephine		Hebrew	God shall add
Josette		French	God shall add
Josie	Jozie	Hebrew	From Josephine, God shall add
Joy		Latin	Joyful
Joyce		Latin	Joyful
Juana		Spanish	God is gracious
Juanita		Spanish	God is gracious
Judith	Judy	Hebrew	Woman from Judea
Juillet		French	July
Jules		Latin	Youthful
Julia		Latin	Youthful
Julie		Latin	Youthful
Juliette		French	Youthful
Jumelle		French	Twin
Justine		Latin	Fair, just
Jyoti		Sanskrit	Light

K

Name	Alternative spellings	Origin	Meaning
Kacie	Kasey, Casey	Irish	Brave
Kadee		Australian	Mother
Kadira		Arabic	Powerful
Kadisha		Hebrew	Holy
Kady		American	Pure
Kaede		Japanese	Maple leaf
Kaela		Arabic	Beloved
Kai		Pacific Islands	Sea
Kaimi		Pacific Islands	The seeker
Kaisa		Scandinavian	Pure
Kaitline	Caitlin	Irish	Pure
Kaiya		Australian	A kind of spear
Kala		Australian	Fire
Kalasia		Pacific Islands	Graceful
Kalei		Pacific Islands	Flower wreath
Kali		Sanskrit	Black
Kalila		Arabic	Beloved
Kalinda		Sanskrit	The sea
Kalisa	Kalissa	American	Blend of Kate and Lisa
Kalpana		Sanskrit	A fantasy
Kalyani		Sanskrit	Lucky, beautiful
Kama		Sanskrit	The golden one
Kamala		Sanskrit	A loin
Kamaria		African	Moonlight
Kameli		Pacific Islands	Honey
Kamil		Arabic	Perfect
Kamilah		Arabic	The perfect one
Kamili		African	Perfection
Kanani		Pacific Islands	Beautiful
Kanti		Sanskrit	Lovely
Kara		Greek	Pure

Name	Alternative spellings	Origin	Meaning
Karen	Karin, Karon, Caron, Caren	Greek	Pure
Karida		Arabic	Virginal
Karima		Arabic	Noble, generous
Karis		Greek	Graceful
Karissa		Greek	Grace
Karita		Scandinavian	Charity
Karlotta		Spanish	Little and strong
Katarina		Scandinavian	Pure
Kate	Cate, Katie	Greek	Pure
Katharina	Katarina	German	Pure
Katharine	Kathy, Kate, Katie, Kath	Greek	Pure
Kathleen	Kathy, Kath	Scottish	Pure
Katinka		Russian	Pure
Katya		Russian	Pure
Kay		Welsh	Joy
Kayla		Hebrew	Like the Lord
Kayleigh		American	Slender
Keana		Irish	Beautiful
Kebira		Arabic	Powerful
Keely	Keeley	Irish	Brave
Keisha		African	Favourite
Kelly		Irish	Intelligent
Kendra		Anglo-Saxon	Knowing
Kenna		American	Good looking
Kenya		Russian	Innocent
Kerensa		Cornish	Loving, affectionate
Kerra		Cornish	Dearer
Kerry	Kerrie, Ceri	Irish	Dark haired, Irish county
Kesare		Spanish	Hairy
Khalida	Khalidah	Arabic	Immortal
Kia		African	Season's beginning
Kiah		Australian	The beautiful place

Name	Alternative spellings	Origin	Meaning
Kiana		American	Ancient
Kiera	Ciara	Irish, Welsh	Little dark one
Kimberley	Kim	Anglo-Saxon	Chief, ruler
Kiri		Pacific Islands	Tree bark
Kirsten		Scandinavian	Follower of Christ
Kirstin		Scottish	Christian
Kirsty	Kirstie	Scottish	Christian
Kit		Greek	Bearer of Christ
Kitten		English	Baby cat
Kodi		American	Helpful
Kohia		Pacific Islands	An exotic flower
Kristen		Scandinavian	Follower of Christ
Krysanthe		Greek	From the flower chrysanthemum
Krystal		American	Clear, brilliant glass
Kumari		Sanskrit	A girl
Kura		Pacific Islands	Red
Kyle		Irish	Attractive
Kylie		Australian	Boomerang
Kyra	Kyri, Kyrie	Greek	Noble

L

Name	Alternative spellings	Origin	Meaning
Lakshmi		Sanskrit	The Hindu goddess of beauty and wealth
Lalita		Sanskrit	Playful, charming
Lamorna		Place name	Cornish fishing village
Lana		Russian	Little rock or handsome
Lani		Pacific Islands	The sky
Lara		Latin	Shining
Larisa	Larissa	Russian	Citadel
Latifa		Arabic	Kind and gentle
Latisha		Latin	Joy
Latoya		Spanish	Victory
Laura		Latin	Crowned with laurels
Laure		French	Crowned with laurels
Laurel		Latin	Crowned with laurels
Lauren		Latin	Crowned with laurels
Lavender		Hebrew	Blue, purple, fragrant flower
Lavinia		Latin	Famous Roman princess
Layla		African	Born at night
Lea		Italian	Weary or ruler
Leaf		Anglo-Saxon	Foliage
Leah		Hebrew	Weary or ruler
Leala		French	Loyal one
Leandra		Latin	Like a lioness

Name	Alternative spellings	Origin	Meaning
Leda		Greek	A queen, mother of Helen of Troy
Lee	Leigh	Anglo-Saxon	From the meadow
Leela		Sanskrit	Playful
Leila		Arabic	Dark as the night
Lelia		Italian	Playful
Lenita		Latin	Gentle
Leona		American	Like a lion
Leonida		Italian	Like a lion
Leonie		Latin	Lioness
Leonoro		Italian	Leader
Leora		Greek	Light
Lesbia		Greek	From the island of Lesbos
Lesley	Leslie	Scottish	From the grey fortress
Letitia		Latin	Happiness
Letizia		Italian	Happy
Lewanna	Lewana	Hebrew	The moon
Lexie		Greek	From Alexis, defender of mankind
Lia		Italian	Hard worker
Liani		Spanish	Youthful
Libby	Libbie	Italian	God is my vow
Libera		Italian	Free
Liberty	Libby	Latin	Free
Libra		Latin	Scales, star sign and constellation
Licia		Italian	From Lisia (in Asia Minor)
Lidia	Lydia	Italian	From Lidia, an ancient region of Asia
Liese		German	God is my vow
Lila	Lyla	Arabic	Night

Name	Alternative spellings	Origin	Meaning
Lilac		Anglo-Saxon	A flower
Lilah		Hebrew	The beautiful temptress
Liliana		Italian	From lily, the flower, symbol of purity and peace
Lilith		Arabic	Dark as night
Lillian		Anglo-Saxon	From the lilac flower
Lilliom		Literary	*Liliom* by Ferenc Molnar
Lily	Lilly	Anglo-Saxon	The flower, symbolic of purity and peace
Lina		Arabic	Tender
Linda		Italian	Pretty girl
Linette		French	A bird
Linn		Anglo-Saxon	Waterfall
Lisa		Hebrew	Consecrated to God
Lisbet	Lisbeth, Lisabetta	Hebrew	Consecrated to God
Lisha		African	Mysterious
Lissa		Greek	Honey bee
Liv		Scandinavian	Life
Livia		Italian	Crown
Liz	Lizzy, Lizzie	Hebrew	Consecrated to God
Liza		Hebrew	Consecrated to God
Lizaveta		Russian	Consecrated to God
Llewella		Welsh	Like a lion
Lois		Anglo-Saxon	Famous warrior
Lona		Spanish	Like a lion
Lorelei		German	Mythical siren of the River Rhine
Lorena		Italian	Laurel
Lorenza		Italian	Crowned with laurels

Name	Alternative spellings	Origin	Meaning
Lori		Latin	Crowned with laurels
Lorna		Literary	*Lorna Doone* by R. D. Blackmore
Lorraine		French	Region of France
Lotte		German	Strong, free
Lotus		Latin	A flower
Louise	Louisa	French	Famous warrior
Lourdes		Spanish	After Lourdes, the famous site of pilgrimage
Love		English	
Loveday		Anglo-Saxon	Love and affection
Lovelace		English	Surname used as a first name
Lovisa		Scandinavian	Famous warrior
Lowenna		Cornish	Joy
Lowri		Welsh	From the laurel tree
Luana		Pacific Islands	Enjoyment
Lucetta		Spanish	Light
Lucia		Italian, Spanish	Light
Luciana	Lucy	Italian	Light
Lucilla	Lucille	Latin	Light
Lucinda	Lucy	Latin	Light
Lucky		American	Fortunate
Lucrezia		Italian	Wealthy
Ludmila		Russian	Favour of the people
Luigia		Italian, Spanish	Famous warrior
Luise		German	Famous warrior
Luisella		Italian	Famous warrior
Lujuana		Spanish	Famous warrior
Lulu		German	Famous warrior
Luna		Latin	The moon
Lunar		Anglo-Saxon	Of the moon

Name	Alternative spellings	Origin	Meaning
Lydia	Lidia	Greek	Woman from Lydia, cultured
Lyla		Arabic	Night
Lyn		Anglo-Saxon	Waterfall
Lynda		Spanish	Pretty
Lyndsey	Lyndsay	Anglo-Saxon	Lincoln's marsh
Lynette		Welsh	Idol
Lynn	Lynne, Lynna	Anglo-Saxon	Waterfall
Lynx		English	Large, wild cat
Lyra		Greek	Lyre player. Star sign and constellation
Lysander	Lysandra	Greek	Liberator
Lyuba		Russian	Love

M

Name	Alternative spellings	Origin	Meaning
Mabel		French	Pretty girl
Macey	Macee, Masey	American	Bitter
Maddalena		Italian	From the village of Magdala
Madelaine	Maddie	Hebrew	From the village of Magdala
Madhuri		Sanskrit	Sweet
Madison		Anglo-Saxon	Son of Matthew
Madonna		Anglo-Saxon	From 'My lady', the Virgin Mary
Madra		Spanish	Mother
Maeve		Irish	Intoxicating. Famous Irish queen
Magda		German	From Mary Magdalene
Magdalene		German	From Mary Magdalene
Magenta		Anglo-Saxon	Deep, bright pink, purple
Maggie	Mags	Greek	Pearl
Mahala		Arabic	Tender
Mahina		Pacific Islands	The moon
Mai		French	May
Maia		Latin	Bitter
Maire		Irish	Bitter
Maisha		African	Life
Maisie		Anglo-Saxon	From Margaret, pearl
Malak		Arabic	An angel
Malati		Sanskrit	A jasmine flower

Name	Alternative spellings	Origin	Meaning
Malaya		Place name	Stems from the Tamil word meaning hill town
Malika		Arabic	Lady, Mistress
Malika		African	Queen
Malory	Mallory	French	Luckless
Mani		Sanskrit	A gem
Manjusha		Sanskrit	A box of jewels
Manon		French	Bitter
Manuela		Italian, Spanish	God is with us
Mara		Latin	Bitter
Marcella		Latin	Of Mars, god of war, warrior
Marcelle		French	Warrior
Marcia		Latin	Of Mars, god of war, warrior
Mardi		French	Tuesday
Mareta	Marita	Italian	Bitter
Margaret	Maggie	Greek	Pearl
Margarita		Greek	Pearl
Margaux		French	Pearl
Margeurite		Latin	Pearl, also a flower
Margot		French	Pearl
Maria	Marie, Mariah	Latin	Bitter
Marian	Marion	Anglo-Saxon	Sea of bitterness
Marianna		Italian	Sea of bitterness
Marianne		French	Bitter
Maribel		Spanish	Blend of Mary and Belle
Marie		French	Bitter
Marigold		Latin	A flower
Marina		Latin	Of the sea
Marine		French	Of the sea
Mariposa		Spanish	Butterfly

Name	Alternative spellings	Origin	Meaning
Mariquita		Spanish	Bitter
Marisa	Marissa	Italian	Bitter
Marita	Mareta	Spanish	Bitter
Mariya	Mariah	Russian	Bitter
Marjorie	Madge, Marj	French	Pearl
Marlene		German	From Mary, bitter and Magdalene
Marlon		Anglo-Saxon	Little hawk
Marna	Marnie	Scandinavian	Of the sea
Marsha		Latin	Of Mars, god of war, warrior
Marta		Italian,	Mistress of the Spanish house
Martha		Anglo-Saxon	Mistress of the house
Martina		Italian	Warrior
Martine		Latin	Of Mars, god of war, warrior
Maru		Pacific Islands	Gentle
Marvelle		French	Miracle
Mary		Latin	Bitter
Maryse		French	Bitter
Marzia		Italian	Bitter
Matana		Arabic	Gift
Mathilde	Mathilda, Tilly	French	Strong in battle
Matilda	Tilly	Anglo-Saxon	Strong in battle
Matilde		Italian	Strong in battle
Maud		Anglo-Saxon	Mightly maiden of battle
Maureen	Mo	Irish	Bitter
Mauve		English	Pale purple
Maxine		Latin	The greatest
Maya		Latin	The great one
Maysa		Arabic	Graceful
McKayla		American	Fiery

Name	Alternative spellings	Origin	Meaning
Medina		Arabic	A city in Saudi Arabia
Medora		Place name	US town
Meena		Sanskrit	Fish
Megan		Irish	Pearl
Melanie	Mel	Greek	Dark one
Melek		Arabic	An angel
Melina		Greek	Gentle
Melinda	Mel	Greek	Honey
Melisenda		Spanish	Honey bee
Melissa		Greek	Honey bee
Melody		Greek	Tune, song
Melosa		Spanish	Honey bee
Mercedes		Spanish	Wages, reward
Meredith		Welsh	Great ruler
Merete		Scandinavian	Pearl
Merise		French	Wild cherry
Meryl		Latin	Blackbird
Mia		Scandinavian	Bitterly wanted child
Michaela		Hebrew	Like the Lord
Michela		Italian	Like God
Michèle		French	Like God
Michelina		Italian	Like God
Michelle		Hebrew	Like the Lord
Micky		Hebrew	Like the Lord
Mignon		French	Petite
Mikhaila		Russian	Like God
Mildred		Anglo-Saxon	Gentle advisor
Milena		Russian	Gracious
Milly	Millie	Anglo-Saxon	From Mildred, gentle advisor
Mina		German	Love
Minerva		Latin	Goddess of wisdom
Mira		Italian	Aim

Name	Alternative spellings	Origin	Meaning
Mirabelle		Latin	Lovely
Miranda		Latin	Admired one
Mirella	Mirelle	Italian	Admired one
Mireya		Spanish	Admired one
Miriam		Latin	Bitter
Misha		Russian	Like God
Mitzi		German	Bitterly wanted child
Mohana		Sanskrit	The enchantress
Moira		Irish	Bitter
Molly		Irish	From Moira, bitter
Mona		Irish	Noble
Money		English	Cash
Monica		Latin	Advisor
Monique		French	Advisor
Montana		Place name	US state
Moon		Anglo-Saxon	Sphere that orbits Earth
Mora	Maura	Spanish	Bitter
Morenwyn		Cornish	Fair maiden
Morgana		Welsh	Bright sea dweller
Morna		Irish	Loved
Morwenna		Cornish	Maiden
Moyna		Irish	Noble
Muna		Arabic	A wish
Munira		Arabic	The luminous one
Muriel		Arabic	Myrhh
Musique		French	Music
Myiesha		Arabic	Life's blessing
Myra		Latin	Fragrant ointment
Myrtle		Greek	Plant name

N

Name	Alternative spellings	Origin	Meaning
Naava		Hebrew	Delightful girl
Nabila		Arabic	Noble
Nada	Nadya, Naadia	Arabic	Generous
Nadia	Naadia, Nadya	Italian	Hope
Nadine	Nadeen	Russian	Dancer
Nadira		Arabic	Precious
Nadya	Nadia, Naadia	Russian	Hope
Nafeeza		Arabic	Precious
Nagini		Sanskrit	Mythical snake-like beauties
Nalini		Sanskrit	Lovely
Nancy		Irish	Generous woman
Nanette		French	Giving
Nani		Pacific Islands	Beautiful
Nanna		Scandinavian	Daring
Naomi		Hebrew	Pleasant
Narcissa		Greek	Self-love
Nastasia		Russian	Resurrection
Natalia		Italian	Born at Christmas
Natalie	Nat	Latin	God's gift
Natascia		Italian	Born at Christmas
Natasha		Russian	Born at Christmas
Nathalie		French	God's gift
Nawal		Arabic	A gift
Nazirah		Arabic	Equal
Nebraska		American	American state
Neera		Italian	From Deyanira, devastating
Nella		Italian	Light of the sun
Nelly		Anglo-Saxon	From Helen, light of the sun
Nereida		Greek	Sea nymph

Name	Alternative spellings	Origin	Meaning
Nerissa		Greek	Sea nymph
Neroli		Greek	Orangle blossom flower
Nerys		Welsh	Noble
Netta		Scottish	Champion
Nettie		French	Gentle
Neva		Spanish	Snow
Nevada		Spanish	Snow-capped
Neve		Italian	Snow
Nia	Nyah	Irish	Beauty, brightness, daughter of Celtic sea god
Niamh		Irish	Beauty, brightness, daughter of Celtic sea god
Nicky	Niki, Nikki	Greek	Victory of the people
Nicola	Nichola	Greek	Victory of the people
Nicole		French	Victory of the people
Nicoletta		Italian	Victory of the people
Nike		Greek	Goddess of victory
Nikita		Greek	Unconquered people
Nimah		Arabic	Blessing
Nina		Hebrew	Beautiful
Nissa		Hebrew	Symbolic
Noelle		French	Christmas
Nola		Latin	Sensual
Noor		Arabic	Light
Nora		Italian	From the north
Noreen		Latin	Acknowledges others
Norma		Anglo-Saxon	From the north

Name	Alternative spellings	Origin	Meaning
Novella		Italian	Daughter of the clouds
Noya		Arabic	Beautiful
Numa		Spanish	Delightful
Nydia		Latin	Home-maker
Nymphadora		Greek	Gift of the nymphs
Nyx		Greek	Lively

O

Name	Alternative spellings	Origin	Meaning
Ocean		Anglo-Saxon	Vast body of water
Océane		French	The ocean
Octavia		Latin	Eighth child
Odessa		Greek	Journey
Odetta		Italian	Wealthy
Odette		French	Wealthy
Ofra	Ofrah	Hebrew	Fawn or lively girl
Ola		Scandinavian	Gold
Olaide		American	Lovely
Olalla		Spanish	Well spoken
Oleander		Greek	A flower
Olga		Italian	Blessed
Olino		Spanish	Scented
Olive		Anglo-Saxon	A tree, colour and food
Olivia		Latin	From the olive tree
Olivie		French	From the olive tree
Olwen		Welsh	Magical
Oma		Arabic	Long-lived
Omesha		African	Splendid
Onda		Italian	Wave
Oni		African	Desired child
Opal		Sanskrit	Precious
Ophelia		Greek	A helper
Ophrah		Hebrew	Fawn or lively girl
Oprah		Greek	Fawn. Name of celebrity chat-show host, Oprah Winfrey
Ora		Pacific Islands, Anglo-Saxon	Life Sea coast
Orana		Australian	The moon
Orene		French	Nurturing
Orin		Welsh	Feisty

Name	Alternative spellings	Origin	Meaning
Orinthia		Literary	*The Apple Cart* by George Bernard Shaw
Orissa		Place name	A region in India
Orla		Irish	Golden princess
Ortensia		Italian	She who is in the garden
Ozara		Hebrew	Treasured

P

Name	Alternative spellings	Origin	Meaning
Pacifica		Spanish	Peaceful
Padma		Sanskrit	A lotus
Page	Paige	French	Sharp
Paisley		Scottish	Patterned
Paka		African	Cat
Palmira		Italian	Palm tree
Paloma		Spanish	Dove
Pamela	Pam	Greek	Sweet as honey
Pandora		Greek	Gifted girl
Pangari		Australian	Soulful
Pansy		Latin	A flower
Paola		Italian	Small
Paradise		English	Perfect place
Paris		Greek	French city
Parminder		Sanskrit	Attractive
Parvati		Sanskrit	The daughter of the mountain
Pascale		French	Born at Easter
Patia		Spanish	Most high
Patience		English	Steady perseverance and even temper
Patricia	Pat, Trish, Trisha	Latin	Noble
Patsy	Pat	Latin	Noble
Paula		Latin	Small
Paulette		French	Small
Pauline		French	Small
Pax		Latin	Goddess of peace
Peace		Anglo-Saxon	Calm or tranquil
Peach		Anglo-Saxon	A fruit
Peaches		Celebrity child	(Paula Yates and Bob Geldof)

Name	Alternative spellings	Origin	Meaning
Pearl		Anglo-Saxon	Luminous jewel found in oyster shells
Pebbles		Anglo-Saxon	Small rounded stones
Peggy		Anglo-Saxon	Pearl
Pelagia		Greek	From the sea
Penelope	Penny	Greek	The weaver
Pepa		Spanish	God will add
Pepita		Spanish	God will add
Peppy		American	From Pepa, God will add
Perla		Spanish, Italian	Pearl
Persia		Place name	Ancient region of the Middle East
Peta		Greek	From Pepita, God will add
Petal		Anglo-Saxon	Part of a flower
Petra		Place name	Ancient city in Jordan
Petronilla		Italian	Yokel
Petula		Anglo-Saxon	Rock
Petunia		Anglo-Saxon	A flower
Philippa	Philly, Pip, Pippa, Pippy	Greek	Lover of horses
Philippine		French	Lover of horses
Philomena		Greek	Lover of the moon
Phoebe		Greek	Light
Phoenix		Greek	Rebirth. Mythical bird who was reborn in fire
Phyliss		Greek	A branch
Phyllida		Greek	Lovely
Pia		Italian	Pious, dutiful
Pierah		Australian	The moon
Pilar		Spanish	Strength
Pink		Anglo-Saxon	A colour

Name	Alternative spellings	Origin	Meaning
Piper		Anglo-Saxon	Pipe player
Pisces		Greek	Fishes. Star sign and constellation
Pixie		Anglo-Saxon	A mythical, mischievous fairylike creature
Plum		Anglo-Saxon	A fruit
Polina		Russian	From the Greek god Apollo
Polly		Anglo-Saxon	From Molly, bitter
Pomona		Latin	Roman goddess of fruit trees
Poppy		Anglo-Saxon	A red flower
Porsche		Latin	Giving, high-minded
Portia	Porscha	Latin	From a Roman tribe
Precious		English	Valuable, beloved
Prema		Sanskrit	Love, affection
Presley		Anglo-Saxon	Priest's meadow
Primrose		Latin	First rose
Princess Tiaamii		Celebrity child	(Katie Price and Peter Andre)
Priscilla		Italian	Ancient
Priya		Sanskrit	Beloved
Providence		Anglo-Saxon	God will provide
Prudence		Latin	Careful
Prunella		Latin	Little plum
Psyche		Greek	Of the soul
Pulika		African	Obedient
Purnima		Sanskrit	The night of the full moon

Q

Name	Alternative spellings	Origin	Meaning
Qadira		Arabic	Powerful
Qamra		Arabic	Moon
Qing		Chinese	Blue
Queenie		Anglo-Saxon	Queen
Quenna		Anglo-Saxon	Queen
Questa		Latin	Seeker
Quinby		Scandinavian	Living like royalty
Quinella		Latin	Twice as pretty
Quisha		African	Spiritual and physical beauty
Quita		Latin	Peaceful

R

Name	Alternative spellings	Origin	Meaning
Rabbit		American	The animal!
Rabi		Arabic	Harvest
Rachael	Rachel	Hebrew	Ewe. Biblical wife of Jacob and mother of Joseph
Radella		Anglo-Saxon	Elfin advisor
Radha		Sanskrit	The name of a Hindu goddess
Rae		Anglo-Saxon	Deer
Rafaella		Hebrew	God has healed
Rafiya		African	Dignified
Rain		Latin	Ruler
Raina		Russian	Queen
Rainbow		English	Arch of colours
Raindrop		Anglo-Saxon	Drop of water that falls from the sky
Raisa		African	Exalted
Raissa		French	Believer
Raja		Arabic	Hope
Rajani		Sanskrit	Dark, of the night
Rakel		Scandinavian	Ewe
Ramona		Anglo-Saxon	Beautiful
Rana		Arabic	Beautiful
Randi	Randy	Anglo-Saxon	Wolf shield
Rangi		Pacific Islands	Heaven
Rani		Sanskrit	A queen
Raphaella		Hebrew	Divine healer
Rashida		Arabic	Righteous
Rati		Sanskrit	Love
Raven		English	Large, black bird
Raya		Russian	Relaxed

Name	Alternative spellings	Origin	Meaning
Razia		Hebrew	Secretive
Rebecca	Rebekah, Becca, Becky	Hebrew	Heifer or knotted chord. Biblical wife of Isaac
Reenie		Greek	Peace-loving
Regina		Latin	Queen, official name of Queen Elizabeth II
Reiko		Japanese	Gratitude
Rena		Hebrew	Song
Renata		Italian	Reborn
Rene		Latin	Reborn
Renée		French	Born again
Renite		Latin	Stubborn
Rewa		Pacific Islands	Slender
Rexanne		Anglo-Saxon	Gracious king
Rhea		Greek	Stream or mother
Rhianna		Welsh	Pure
Rhiannon		Welsh	Nymph, goddess
Rhoda		Greek	Rose
Rhonda		Place name	Rhonda valley in Wales
Rhonwen		Welsh	Fair haired
Ria		Spanish	River
Rica		Spanish	Celestial
Richelle		American	From the word rich
Ridhaa		African	Goodwill
Rina	Rinah	Hebrew	Complete joy
Ripple		Anglo-Saxon	Disturbance in smooth water
Rita		Italian	From Margarita, pearl
Riva		Italian	Shore
Roberta		Italian	Bright fame
Robin	Robyn	Anglo-Saxon	Bright fame

Name	Alternative spellings	Origin	Meaning
Robina		Italian	Bright fame
Roche		French	Rock
Rochelle		French	Little rock
Rohana		Sanskrit	Sandalwood
Roisin		Irish	Rose
Roksana		Russian	Dawn
Romilda		Italian	Heroine
Romilly		Latin	Wanderer
Romola		Italian	From Romilia
Romy		German	From Rosemary, from the herb
Rona		Scandinavian	Mighty power
Ros		Irish	Rose
Rosa		Latin	Rose
Rosalia	Rosa, Roz	Latin	Beautiful rose
Rosalie	Rosa, Roz	Latin	Beautiful rose
Rosalind	Rosa, Roz	Latin	Beautiful rose
Rosalyn	Roz	Latin	Beautiful rose
Rosamond	Rosamund	Latin	Pure rose
Rosanna	Rossana	Italian	Rose, grace
Rosaria		Italian	Rosary
Rosario		Spanish	Rosary
Rose		Latin	The flower
Rosemary		Latin	From the herb
Rosenwyn		Cornish	Fair rose
Rosetta		Italian	Rose
Rosie		Latin	The flower
Rosina		Italian	Rose
Rosita		Italian, Spanish	Rose
Rosslyn		Welsh	Moorland lake
Rowena		Latin	From the Rowan tree
Roxanna	Roxana, Roxy	Arabic	Beautiful dawn
Roxanne	Roxy	Arabic	Beautiful dawn
Royale		French	Regal
Rubena		Hebrew	See, a son

Name	Alternative spellings	Origin	Meaning
Ruby		Latin	Red, precious stone
Rudy		German	Sly
Rue		English	Regret
Rufina		Italian	Red haired
Rukmini		Sanskrit	The wife of Lord Krishna
Rula		Russian	Sovereign
Runa		Scandinavian	Secret lore
Ruth		Hebrew	Beautiful and compassionate

S

Name	Alternative spellings	Origin	Meaning
Saada		African	Helper
Sabah		Arabic	Morning
Sabbia		Italian	Sand
Sabina	Sabine	Latin	From the Sabine tribe from Roman Italy
Sabira	Sabirah	Arabic	Patience
Sabra		African	Patience
Sabrina		Welsh	In Celtic legend the girl who gave her name to the River Severn
Sacha	Sasha	Russian	Defender of mankind
Sadhbh		Irish	Sweet
Sadie		Hebrew	Princess
Safari		African	Long journey
Saffron		Arabic	A spice
Safia		Arabic	Pure one
Safran		French	Saffron
Saga		Scandinavian	Sensual
Sahar		Arabic	Dawn
Sahara		Arabic	Desert
Saida		Arabic	Lucky
Saison		French	Season
Sakinah		Arabic	Divine tranquillity
Salima	Salimah, Salma, Selma, Zelma	Arabic	Safe
Sally		Hebrew	Princess
Salome		Hebrew	Peace
Salvadora		Spanish	Saved
Salwa		Arabic	Comfort

Name	Alternative spellings	Origin	Meaning
Samantha	Sam, Sammy	Greek	Listener of God
Samara		Hebrew	Guarded by God
Samirah		Arabic	Lively companion
Samma		Arabic	Sky
Samuela		Hebrew	God has heard
Sana		Arabic	Radiant
Sandia		Spanish	Defender of mankind
Sandra		Italian	Defender of mankind
Sandrea		Greek	Defender of mankind
Sandy	Sandie	Greek	Defender of mankind
Sanila		Sanskrit	Full of praise
Santa		Italian	Saintly
Santina		Italian	Saintly
Sapphire		Greek	A precious deep blue gem
Sara		Italian	Princess
Sarah		Hebrew	A princess. Abraham's wife in the Bible
Saree		Arabic	Noble
Sarisha		Sanskrit	Charming
Saroja		Sanskrit	Born in a lake
Sasha		Russian	Defender of mankind
Saskia		Scandinavian	Defender of mankind
Sassa		Scandinavian	Divine beauty
Satine	Satin	French	Shining
Savanna		Spanish	Grassy plain
Savannah		Place name	US city
Sawsan		Arabic	Lily of the valley

Name	Alternative spellings	Origin	Meaning
Scarlet		Anglo-Saxon	Deep, dark red
Scout		Celebrity child	(Demi Moore and Bruce Willis)
Sea		American	Salt water, large expanse
Sean		Irish	God is gracious
Seema		Hebrew	Treasured
Selena	Selina, Selene	Greek	Goddess of the moon
Senara		Cornish	From St Zennor
Serena		Latin	Calm, serene
Serendipity		English	Making lucky discoveries by accident
Serenity		Latin	Calm, peaceful
Sevilla		Spanish	From Seville
Shadow		English	
Shae		Hebrew	Sky
Shahira		Arabic	Famous
Shakira		Arabic	Thankful
Shakti		Sanskrit	The powerful one
Shakuntala		Sanskrit	A bird
Shamra		Sanskrit	Adorable
Shance		French	Grateful
Shane		Irish	God is gracious
Shania		American	Native American for 'on my way'
Shannon		Irish	God is gracious
Shanti		Sanskrit	The tranquil one
Sharmila		Sanskrit	The protected one
Sharon		Hebrew	A flat plain
Shauny		Irish	God is gracious
Shavon		Irish	Devout
Shawnee		American	Native American Indian tribe

Name	Alternative spellings	Origin	Meaning
Shea		Irish	Soft beauty
Sheela		Sanskrit	Of good character
Sheena		Hebrew	God is gracious
Sheila		Latin	Blind
Shelah		Hebrew	Request
Shelby		Anglo-Saxon	Sheltered town
Shelley		Anglo-Saxon	From the meadow on the ledge
Sher		Sanskrit	The beloved one
Sherilyn		American	Blend of Cheryl and Marilyn
Sheronne	Sherron	Hebrew	From Sharon, fertile plain
Sheryl		French	Beloved
Shine		American	To glow
Shira		Hebrew	My song
Shirley		Anglo-Saxon	Willow farm
Shobhana		Sanskrit	The beautiful one
Shona		Irish	God is gracious
Shukuma		African	Be thankful
Sian		Irish	God is gracious
Sieglind		German	Tender victory
Siena	Sienna	Italian	Italian city
Sierra		Latin	From the mountains
Sigourney		French	Daring king
Sigrid		Scandinavian	Beautiful victory
Silje		Scandinavian	Blind one
Silke		German	Blind one
Silvana		Italian	From the forest
Silver		Anglo-Saxon	Lustrous
Silvia	Sylvia	Italian	From the forest
Simona		Italian	The listener

Name	Alternative spellings	Origin	Meaning
Simone		Hebrew	The listener
Sine		Irish	God is gracious
Sinead		Irish	God is gracious
Siobhan		Irish	God is gracious
Siren		Greek	Beautiful mythical women who lured sailors into the sea
Siri		Scandinavian	Beautiful victory
Sisi		African	Born on Sunday
Sissel		Scandinavian	Blind one
Sissy	Cissy, Cicely	Anglo-Saxon	Blind one
Sita		Sanskrit	The Hindu goddess of the harvest
Sitara		Sanskrit	Morning star
Siti		African	Lady
Siv		Scandinavian	Bride
Sky		Anglo-Saxon	Space above the ground
Skye		Place name	Isle of Skye in Scotland
Snow		Anglo-Saxon	Frozen water that falls from the sky
Snowflake		Anglo-Saxon	Ice crystals that fall from the sky
Socorro		Spanish	Helpful
Sofia		Italian	Wisdom
Sofiya		Russian	Wisdom
Solana		Spanish	Sunlight and eastern breeze
Soleil		French	Sun
Song		Anglo-Saxon	A piece of music
Sonia	Sonya	Anglo-Saxon	Wisdom
Sonora		Celebrity child	(Alice and Sheryl Cooper)

Name	Alternative spellings	Origin	Meaning
Sonya	Sonia	Russian	Wisdom
Sophia		Latin	Wisdom
Sophie		French	Wisdom
Soraya		Arabian	Weatlh, riches
Sorcha		Irish	Shining
Sorrel		English	Plant name
Spring		Anglo-Saxon	Season before summer
Stacey		Latin	Prosperous
Stasya		Russian	Resurrection
Stefania		Italian	Crown
Stefanie	Stef, Steffie	German	Crown
Stella		Latin	A star
Stephanie		Greek	Crown
Stevie		Greek	A crown
Storm		Anglo-Saxon	Thunder and lightning
Sue		Hebrew	From Susan, lily
Sugar		English	Sweet crystals obtained from cane or beet
Sujata		Sanskrit	Of noble birth
Suki		Japanese	Beloved
Sultana		Arabic	Queen
Sumehra		Arabic	Beautiful face
Summer		Anglo-Saxon	The hottest season
Sunita		Sanskrit	Of good conduct
Sunn		Anglo-Saxon	Cheerful
Sunniva		Anglo-Saxon	Gift of the sun
Sunset		Anglo-Saxon	Time the sun disappears below the horizon
Sunshine		Anglo-Saxon	Warmth and light of the sun
Susan	Sue, Susie, Suzie	Hebrew	A lily

Name	Alternative spellings	Origin	Meaning
Susanna	Sue, Susie, Suzie	Italian	A lily
Susannah	Sue, Susie, Suzie	Hebrew	A lily
Susanne	Sue, Susie, Suzie	French	A lily
Sveta		Russian	Light
Svetlana		Russian	Light
Swan		English	White, graceful bird
Sweetie		English	Cute
Sybil	Cybil	Greek	Mythical prophet
Sydney		Place name	City in Australia
Sylvia	Silvia	Latin	From the woods
Sylvie		French	From the woods
Symphony		Latin	A piece of music

T

Name	Alternative spellings	Origin	Meaning
Tabita		African	Graceful
Tabitha	Tabby	Greek	Gazelle
Taffeta		American	Shiny material
Taffy		Welsh	Beloved
Tahira	Tahirah	Arabic	Virtuous
Talibah		African	Intelligent
Tallara		Australian	Rain
Tallulah		Irish	Wealthy princess. Character in the play *Bugsy Malone*
Talwyn		Cornish	Fair brow
Tamara		Hebrew	A palm tree
Tamika		African	Lively
Tamsin	Tammy	Anglo-Saxon	Benevolent
Tangelina		Greek	Angel
Tanya	Tania	Russian	Derived from Roman family name Tatius
Tara		Irish	Irish place name, seat of the high kings
Tarana		Australian	A large waterhole
Tasha	Tash	Russian	From Natasha, born at Christmas
Tate	Tait	Anglo-Saxon	Bringer of joy
Tathra		Australian	Beautiful countryside
Tatum		Anglo-Saxon	Bringer of joy
Tawia		African	Born after twins
Taylor		Anglo-Saxon	Cutter, person who makes clothes

Name	Alternative spellings	Origin	Meaning
Tegen	Teagan, Teagen	Welsh, Cornish	Pretty little thing
Tempest		French	Tempestuous
Tennessee		Place name	US state. First name of author Tennessee Williams
Teresa	Terry, Teri, Theresa	Greek	Reaper
Terra		Latin	Earth
Terri	Teri, Terry	Greek	Reaper
Tess		Greek	Reaper
Tessa		Greek	Reaper
Thada		Greek	Thankful
Thalia		Greek	Legendary muse of comedy
Thana		Arabic	Thankful
Thara		Arabic	Wealthy
Thelma		Greek	A wish
Theodora	Theo	Greek	Gift of God
Thérèse		French	Reaper
Theta		Greek	Substantial
Thomasina		Greek	A twin
Thora		Scandinavian	From Norse god of thunder, Thor
Tia		Spanish	Princess
Tiara		Latin	Three-tiered crown
Tibby		American	From Tabitha, gazelle
Tierra		Spanish	Earth
Tiffany		Greek	Revelation of God
Tigerlily		Celebrity child	(Paula Yates and Michael Hutchence)

Name	Alternative spellings	Origin	Meaning
Tilda	Tilde	Scandinavian	Mighty battle
Tilly		German	From Matilda, strong in battle
Tina		Latin	Little
Tirranna		Australian	Running water
Tisha		African	Determined
Titania		Greek	Great one. Fairy Queen in *A Midsummer Night's Dream*
Tiziana		Italian	Great one
Toby	Tobie	Latin	God is good
Toffey		American	From the sweet, toffee
Tony	Toni, Tonie	Latin	Worthy of praise
Topaz		Sanskrit	Fire
Tora		Scandinavian	Thunder
Tordis		Scandinavian	Goddess, taken from Thor, Norse god of thunder
Tori	Tory	Latin	From Victoria, winner
Tracey	Tracy	Gaelic	Fighter
Tree		English	Strong plant with woody main stem or trunk
Tricia	Trish, Trisha	Latin	From Patricia, noble
Trina		Greek	Pure. From Katrina
Trinity		Latin	A trio
Trista		Latin	Melancholy one
Trixie	Trixee	Latin	From Beatrix, voyager

Name	Alternative spellings	Origin	Meaning
Trotula		Italian	From famous female doctor Trotula of Salemo
Trudy	Trude, Truda	German	From Gerturde, strong, spear, or Ermentrude, whole, strong
True		American	Honest
Truly		American	Honestly
Tulia		Spanish	Glorious
Tullia		Italian	Heavy rain
Tully		Irish	Powerful
Turin		Place name	Italian town
Turua		Pacific Islands	Beautiful
Twiggy		English	Like a twig
Tyne		Place name	English river
Tyra		Scandinavian	Assertive

U

Name	Alternative spellings	Origin	Meaning
Uda		German	Prosperous
Udele		Anglo-Saxon	Wealthy
Ula		Welsh	Jewel of the sea
Ulani		Pacific Islands	Happy
Ulima		Arabic	Wise
Ulla		Australian	A well
Ulrika		Scandinavian	Wealthy and powerful
Uma		Sanskrit	Light, peace
Umar		Arabic	Flourishing
Umina		Australian	Sleep
Unicorn		English	Mythical horse-like creature with a horn
Unique		English	One of a kind
Unity		Latin	United
Urania		Greek	Heavenly
Ursa		Greek	Bear. Name of Ursa major and minor constellations
Ursula		Hebrew	A bear
Usha		Sanskrit	The dawn
Uta		German	Rich
Utopia		Greek	Perfect place
Uzima		African	Vitality
Uzuri		African	Beauty

V

Name	Alternative spellings	Origin	Meaning
Vala		Italian	Singled out
Valentina		Italian	Healthy, right for marriage
Valentine		Latin	Healthy, also the patron saint of lovers
Valérie		French	Brave, courageous
Valeska		Russian	Glorious ruler
Valletta		Place name	City in Malta
Valma		Welsh	Mayflower
Vanessa		Literary	*Gulliver's Travels* by Jonathan Swift's
Vanna		Russian	God is gracious
Vasanti		Sanskrit	Spring
Veda		Sanskrit	Wisdom and knowledge
Vega		Arabic	Falling. A star in the Lyra constellation
Velma		American	Wilful, determined
Velvet		English	Soft material
Venice		Place name	Italian city
Ventura		Spanish	The future
Venus		Latin	Roman goddess of beauty and love
Vera		Latin	Truth
Verity		Latin	Truth
Verona		Place name	Italian city
Veronica		Latin	True likeness
Véronique		French	True likeness
Vesta		Greek	Goddess of fire and the hearth
Vic		Latin	Victor, winner
Vicky	Vicki, Viki, Vikki	Latin	From Victoria, victor, winner

Name	Alternative spellings	Origin	Meaning
Victoire		French	Winner
Victoria	Vicky, Vicki, Viki, Vikki, Tory, Vic	Latin	Victor, winner
Vida		Latin	The beloved one
Vidya		Sanskrit	Knowledge
Villette		French	From the village
Vimala		Sanskrit	Pure
Vina		Spanish	Vineyard
Viola		Italian	Violet
Violanda		Italian	Violet
Violet		Latin	A purple flower
Violetta		Italian	Violet
Virdis		Latin	Fresh, blooming
Virginia		Latin	Chaste, pure
Virginie	Ginny	French	Pure, chaste
Virgo		Latin	Virgin, maiden. Star sign and constellation
Vita		Italian	Life
Vittoria	Vitoria	Italian, Spanish	Winner
Vivian	Vivienne	Latin	Lively
Viviana		Italian	Lively
Vivienne	Vivian	French	Lively
Vladisalva		Russian	To rule with glory
Vladmira		Russian	To rule with greatness
Volante		Latin	The flying one
Voletta		French	Veiled
Vonda		Russian	Of the Wend people

W

Name	Alternative spellings	Origin	Meaning
Wahiba		Arabic	Generous
Wahida		Arabic	Unique
Walida		Arabic	The newborn girl
Wallis		Anglo-Saxon	Stranger
Wanda		Anglo-Saxon	Young tree
Wangari		African	Leopard
Wasima		Arabic	Graceful, pretty
Wendelin		German	Of the Wend people
Wendy		Literary	*Peter Pan* by J. M. Barrie
Wenna		Cornish	From St Wenn
Whitney		Anglo-Saxon	From the white island
Widjan		Arabic	Bliss
Wilda		Anglo-Saxon	Wild
Wilhelmina		German	Strong protector
Willa		Anglo-Saxon	Determined
Willow		Anglo-Saxon	From willow tree
Wilma		German	Strong protector
Wilona		Anglo-Saxon	Hoped for
Winifred	Winnie	Anglo-Saxon	Blessed peacemaker
Winky		Literary	House elf in the Harry Potter books
Winna		African	Friend
Winnie		Anglo-Saxon	Blessed peacemaker
Winola		German	Gracious friend
Winona	Winnie	American	American Indian for oldest daughter
Winsome		Anglo-Saxon	Pleasant
Wren		English	Small bird
Wylda		German	Rebellious

X

Name	Alternative spellings	Origin	Meaning
Xaviera		Italian, Spanish	Luminous
Xena		Greek	Quest
Xiomara		Spanish	Quest
Xuxa		Spanish	Lily
Xylia		Spanish	Woodland dweller

Y

Name	Alternative spellings	Origin	Meaning
Yaa		African	Born on Thursday
Yaffa		Hebrew	Beautiful
Yakini		African	Truth
Yancey		American	From the term Yankee
Yani		Australian	Peace
Yara		Australian	A kind of bird
Yaromira		Russian	A great spring
Yasmina		Arabic	Jasmine flower
Yeira		Hebrew	Light
Yelena		Russian	Light of the sun
Yindi		Australian	Sun
Yoko		Japanese	Four, positive, side. Yoko Ono, John Lennon's wife
Yolanda		Greek	Violet flower
Yomaris		Spanish	I am the sun
Yoshiko		Japanese	Good child
Yovela		Hebrew	Rejoicing
Ysella		Cornish	Modest
Ysobel		Spanish	Consecrated to God
Yusra		Arabic	Wealthy
Yvonne		French	Young archer

Z

Name	Alternative spellings	Origin	Meaning
Zabrina		Anglo-Saxon	Noble maiden
Zada	Zaida	Arabic	Lucky
Zadie		Arabic	From Zaida, prosperous
Zafiro		Spanish	Sapphire
Zahara	Zahra	Arabic	A flower
Zaina		Arabic	Beautiful
Zakira		Arabic	God has remembered
Zalika		African	Well born
Zara		Hebrew	The bright dawn
Zarifa		Arabic	Graceful
Zawadi		African	Gift
Zebada		Hebrew	The Lord's gift
Zelda		Anglo-Saxon	Companion
Zelia		Greek	Zealous, dutiful
Zelma		Literary	Beautiful appearance
Zena		Greek	Hospitable
Zenith		Arabic	The highest point
Zennor		Place name	Cornish village
Zera		Greek	Seeds
Zhenya		Russian	Of good birth
Zia		Arabic	Splendour
Zina		Russian	Shining or sky
Zinaida		Russian	Shining or sky
Zinovia		Russian	Life of Zeus
Ziona		Hebrew	A sign
Zita		Latin	Patron saint of domestic servants
Ziva		Hebrew	Brightness
Zoe		Greek	Life
Zohara		Hebrew	The bright child
Zohra		Arabic	Blossoming

Name	Alternative spellings	Origin	Meaning
Zola		Latin	Earth
Zora		Latin	The dawn
Zulema		Arabic	Peace
Zuwina		African	Good

3

Twenty-five lists to inspire you

1. Latin names

BOYS

Adrian	Claude	Gilderoy
Alban	Clement	Guy
Albion	Cornelius	Hilary
Albus	Crispin	Horace
Amadeus	Cupid	Horatio
Anthony	Dean	Jet
Aurelius	Deo	Jove
Ben	Dexter	Judd
Benedict	Dominic	Jules
Benjamin	Draco	Julius
Bennet	Emil	Justin
Bennett	Errol	Justus
Benson	Fabian	Krispin
Blaise	Faustus	Lacy
Calvin	Felix	Larry
Cassius	Festus	Laurence
Cecil	Fidel	Laurie
Chester	Figaro	Lawrence
Christian	Filius	Leo
Cicero	Firenze	Lèon
Clarence	Francis	Lionel
Clark	Frankie	Lorimer

Lucian	Patrick	Terry
Lucius	Paul	Tivon
Ludo	Peregrine	Tobias
Marc	Phineas	Tobie
Marcus	Placido	Toby
Mark	Primo	Todd
Martin	Prince	Tony
Maurice	Quentin	Torrence
Mayer	Quincy	Trent
Miles	Rebel	Turner
Morris	Remus	Urban
Mundungus	Rex	Usher
Myles	Romeo	Valentine
Mylo	Rufus	Vernon
Nemo	Salazar	Vic
Nero	Sebastian	Victor
Nigel	Severus	Vidal
Nimrod	Silas	Vince
Octavius	Silvester	Vincent
Oliver	Sirius	Vinnie
Orsen	Sol	Virgil
Paddy	Sylvester	Voldemort
Pascal	Tarquin	
Pat	Terence	

GIRLS

Adriana	Beatrice	Cassia
Alida	Begonia	Cecilia
Amity	Bellatrix	Celeste
Anabelle	Benedicta	Charity
Antonia	Brittany	Charmaine
April	Camelia	Chastity
Arabella	Camilla	Chris
Aria	Camille	Christina
Ariana	Candice	Claire
Aurelia	Carissa	Clarice
Barbara	Carmel	Clarissa

Claudia	Jill	Meryl
Connie	Jillian	Minerva
Coral	Joquil	Mirabelle
Cornelia	Joy	Miranda
Crisanta	Joyce	Miriam
Cybill	Jules	Monica
Dahlia	Julia	Myra
Delphine	Julie	Nat
Delphinium	Justine	Natalie
Demi	Lara	Nola
Diana	Latisha	Noreen
Dinah	Laura	Nydia
Drusilla	Laurel	Octavia
Dulcie	Lauren	Olivia
Erma	Lavinia	Pansy
Estelle	Leandra	Pat
Felicia	Lenita	Patricia
Felicity	Leonie	Patsy
Felita	Letitia	Paula
Fleur	Liberty	Pax
Flora	Lori	Pomona
Florence	Lotus	Porsche
Florida	Lucilla	Portia
Frances	Lucinda	Primrose
Frankie	Lucy	Prudence
Gardenia	Luna	Prunella
Gazelle	Maia	Questa
Gemma	Mara	Quinella
Gill	Marcella	Quita
Gillian	Marcia	Rain
Ginny	Margeurite	Regina
Gloria	Maria	Rene
Grace	Marigold	Renite
Hilary	Marina	Romilly
Honour	Marsha	Rosa
Hyacinth	Martine	Rosalia
Imogen	Mary	Rosalie
Irma	Maxine	Rosalind

Rosalyn	Sylvia	Veronica
Rosamond	Symphony	Vic
Rose	Terra	Vicky
Rosemary	Tina	Victoria
Rosie	Toby	Vida
Rowena	Tony	Viki
Ruby	Tori	Violet
Sabina	Tricia	Virdis
Sabine	Trinity	Virginia
Serena	Trisha	Vivian
Serenity	Trista	Volante
Sheila	Unity	Zita
Sierra	Valentine	Zola
Sophia	Venus	Zora
Stacey	Vera	
Stella	Verity	

2. Greek names

BOYS

Achilles
Adonis
Ajax
Alex
Alexander
Alexis
Ambrose
Anatole
Andrew
Apollo
Arcadio
Archimedes
Argus
Arion
Aristo
Artemas
Athan
Balthasar
Balthazar
Barnabas
Barnaby
Basil
Christopher
Cosmo
Cyril
Damien
Darien
Darius
Deacon
Dedalus
Dennis
Drew

Erasmus
Eros
Eugene
Eustace
Galen
Gene
George
Giles
Gregory
Griffin
Hagrid
Hector
Hercules
Hermes
Jason
Jerome
Kit
Kristopher
Leander
Linus
Luke
Lysander
Magnus
Neo
Nestor
Nicholas
Nike
Ocean
Otis
Palladin
Par
Paris

Peter
Philip
Philo
Phoenix
Piers
Pip
Rubeus
Sandy
Stacey
Stavros
Stelios
Stephen
Steven
Thaddeus
Theo
Theodore
Theron
Thomas
Tim
Timothy
Titan
Tom
Tommy
Tomo
Ulysses
Xander
Xanthus
Xeno
Yannis
Zander
Zeth
Zeus

GIRLS

Adelpha
Agape
Agatha
Agnes
Alanis
Alessandra
Alethea
Alex
Alexandra
Alexis
Alice
Alicia
Alison
Alyssa
Amara
Amaryllis
Aminta
Andrea
Andy
Angela
Angelica
Aphrodite
Araminta
Aretha
Asia
Asta
Astra
Athena
Aura
Ava
Azalea
Berenice
Beryl
Bryony
Calla
Callidora

Callista
Calypso
Cassandra
Catherine
Celene
Celina
Celine
Charis
Charisma
Charissa
Chloe
Chrysilla
Cilla
Cindy
Cleo
Clio
Cora
Cosima
Crystal
Cynthia
Damara
Daphne
Daria
Deianeira
Dell
Della
Denise
Dido
Dione
Dora
Dorian
Doris
Dorothy
Drew
Ebony
Echo

Effie
Elaine
Eleanor
Electra
Ellie
Eudora
Eunice
Eustacia
Evangelia
Gaea
Gaia
Georgia
Georgina
Gina
Greer
Harmony
Helen
Hermione
Hypatia
Ianthe
Iola
Iolanthe
Irene
Iris
Isadora
Jacaranda
Jacinda
Kara
Karen
Karis
Karissa
Kate
Katharine
Kit
Krysanthe
Kyra

Leda
Leora
Lesbia
Lexie
Lissa
Lydia
Lyra
Lysander
Lysandra
Maggie
Margaret
Melanie
Melina
Melinda
Melissa
Melody
Myrtle
Narcissa
Nereida
Nerissa
Neroli
Nicky
Nicola
Nike
Nikita
Nymphadora
Nyx
Odessa

Oleander
Ophelia
Oprah
Pamela
Pandora
Paris
Pelagia
Penelope
Penny
Peta
Philippa
Philly
Philomena
Phoebe
Phoenix
Phyliss
Phyllida
Pippa
Psyche
Reenie
Rhea
Rhoda
Samantha
Sandrea
Sandy
Sapphire
Selena
Selene

Stephanie
Stevie
Sybil
Tabitha
Tangelina
Teresa
Terri
Tess
Tessa
Thada
Thalia
Thelma
Theodora
Theta
Thomasina
Tiffany
Titania
Trina
Urania
Vesta
Xena
Yolanda
Zelia
Zena
Zera
Zoe

3. Anglo-Saxon names

BOYS

Ainsley
Albert
Alden
Aldon
Aldwin
Alfie
Alfred
Algar
Alger
Alvin
Alwyn
Armstrong
Ash
Ashley
Aston
Aubrey
Auden
Avery
Barclay
Barney
Baron
Bartemius
Bartholomew
Barton
Baxter
Beethoven
Bernard
Bertram
Bill
Billy
Blake
Bobby
Bond

Bosley
Bradford
Brandon
Branson
Brock
Bron
Bronson
Bronze
Brook
Brown
Bud
Buddy
Byron
Carrington
Chad
Chandler
Chopin
Cirrus
Cliff
Clifford
Clint
Clinton
Clive
Cloud
Cody
Colby
Cooper
Courtney
Curtis
Cuthbert
Cyclone
Darren
Dell

Denby
Denton
Digby
Dudley
Durwin
Durwyn
Dustin
Earl
Eddison
Edgar
Edmund
Edward
Edwin
Eldon
Eldrid
Eldwyn
Elmer
Elton
Elvis
Emmet
Eric
Esmond
Evelyn
Farley
Ferdinand
Fire
Flame
Floyd
Foley
Ford
Forest
Fowler
Frank

Franklin
Fred
Frederick
Freeman
Geoff
Geoffrey
Gerald
Gerard
Gladwyn
Godric
Gordon
Graham
Guillaume
Hail
Hamilton
Harrison
Harry
Hartley
Hayward
Heath
Henderson
Henry
Hilton
Holden
Holder
Hugh
Hurricane
Huxley
Ice
Ingram
Irwin
Ivor
Jack
Jackson
Jagger
Jaimie
James
Jarvis

Jasper
Jeffrey
Jeremy
Jevon
Jim
Jools
Kendall
Kim
King
Kinglsey
Kipp
Kirby
Knox
Lance
Lane
Langley
Leaf
Lee
Leighton
Lester
Lewis
Linford
Lyman
Lyndon
Lindsey
Mallory
Manfred
Marley
Marvin
Maxwell
Maynard
Melbourne
Merton
Milburn
Morrissey
Morton
Ned
Nellie

Newton
Nixon
Norman
Norton
Norward
Oakley
Odin
Ogden
Onslow
Orme
Orvin
Orvyn
Osborne
Osburt
Osgood
Osmond
Oswald
Palmer
Parker
Patton
Paxton
Pearson
Piper
Pollock
Presley
Preston
Radley
Ralph
Ramsey
Randolf
Randolph
Randy
Red
Reeve
Richard
Ridgley
Ripple
Robert

Robin	Shelley	Tyler
Robson	Sherwin	Umber
Rochester	Sherwyn	Vance
Rock	Shipley	Vere
Rocky	Sinclair	Wallace
Roderick	Sinjon	Wallis
Roland	Slade	Walter
Rowan	Smith	Warren
Royce	Smokey	Wayne
Royston	Stanley	Webster
Rudd	Starr	Wilbur
Russell	Stewart	Wilfred
Rusty	Storm	William
Rutledge	Stuart	Willis
Sanders	Sumner	Wilson
Sanford	Tate	Winston
Saxon	Taylor	Woodrow
Scott	Ted	Woody
Selwin	Thane	Worth
Selwyn	Theobald	Wycliff
Shamrock	Tor	Wynne
Shandy	Travis	Yardley
Shelby	Truman	
Sheldon	Tucker	

GIRLS

Acorn	Bluebell	Crystal
Alberta	Blythe	Daisy
Apple	Bobby	Dandelion
Ash	Bonnie	Darcy
Ashley	Bramble	Dawn
Audrey	Brook	Dusk
Autumn	Carole	Eartha
Beatrix	Chelsea	Edith
Berry	Cirrus	Edwina
Billie	Cloud	Elvina
Blossom	Clover	Elwyn

Elysia	Magenta	Rexanne
Ethel	Maisie	Ripple
Etta	Marian	Robin
Fay	Martha	Scarlet
Fen	Matilda	Shelby
Fern	Maud	Shelley
Godiva	Mildred	Shirley
Goldie	Milly	Silver
Halle	Moon	Sissy
Hayley	Nelly	Sky
Hazel	Norma	Snow
Heather	Ocean	Snowflake
Helga	Olive	Song
Hester	Ora	Spring
Holly	Peace	Storm
Ivy	Peach	Summer
Jada	Pearl	Sunn
Jade	Pebbles	Sunniva
Joan	Peggy	Sunset
Kendra	Petal	Sunshine
Kim	Petula	Tamsin
Kimberley	Petunia	Tate
Leaf	Pink	Tatum
Lee	Piper	Taylor
Leigh	Pixie	Udele
Lilac	Plum	Wallis
Lillian	Polly	Wanda
Lily	Poppy	Whitney
Linn	Presley	Wilda
Lois	Providence	Willa
Loveday	Queenie	Willow
Lunar	Quenna	Wilona
Lyn	Radella	Winifred
Lyndsey	Rae	Winnie
Lynn	Raindrop	Winsome
Madison	Ramona	Zabrina
Madonna	Randi	Zelda

4. Irish names

BOYS

Aidan	Darragh	Harvey
Alan	Darrick	Hurley
Alister	Dary	Innis
Allan	Declan	Jackie
Bairrie	Delaney	Kane
Barry	Dempsey	Kasey
Blaine	Dermot	Keagan
Blair	Desmond	Kean
Blayney	Devin	Keanan
Brendan	Devlyn	Kearney
Brian	Diarmaid	Keefe
Broderick	Donovan	Keegan
Brody	Doyle	Keenan
Bryan	Drake	Kelly
Cal	Dwayne	Kelvin
Callum	Dwyer	Ken
Carbry	Eamon	Kendrick
Casey	Erin	Kennedy
Cassidy	Farrell	Kenneth
Clancy	Fearghal	Kevin
Codie	Ferghus	Kieran
Cody	Fergus	Lennon
Coleman	Ferguson	Liam
Colin	Finbar	Logan
Colm	Findlay	Maclain
Conan	Finlay	Mahoney
Conn	Finn	Malone
Conor	Finnegan	Melvin
Corey	Flannagan	Monroe
Cormac	Flynn	Neal
Daley	Gallagher	Niall
Darcy	Guthne	Nolan
Daric	Haley	Nyle

Orran
Quinn
Reagan
Regan
Rehgan
Riley
Roark
Roary
Ronan
Rorke

Ryan
Scanlan
Seamus
Sean
Shaine
Shamus
Shane
Shannon
Shaun
Shauny

Shayne
Sullivan
Sweeney
Tiernan
Trevor
Troy
Tuily
Tyrone

GIRLS

Adan
Aidan
Aine
Aiofe
Aislin
Aithne
Alana
Alannah
Alayna
Blaine
Bridget
Brighid
Brigid
Caitlin
Caoimhe
Casey
Colleen
Corey
Dana
Deirdre
Dervla
Doherty
Eileen

Ena
Erin
Grainne
Granya
Ina
Kacie
Kaitline
Keana
Keely
Kelly
Kerry
Kiera
Kyle
Maeve
Maire
Maureen
Megan
Moira
Molly
Mona
Morna
Moyna
Nancy

Nia
Niamh
Orla
Roisin
Ros
Sadhbh
Sean
Shane
Shannon
Shauny
Shavon
Shea
Shona
Sian
Sine
Sinead
Siobhan
Sorcha
Tallulah
Tara
Tully

5. Welsh names

BOYS

Aled	Cai	Keith
Alun	Caio	Kent
Anwell	Caradoc	Kirwyn
Anwyl	Caradwg	Lincoln
Arlin	Cary	Llewelyn
Arthur	Ciaran	Lloyd
Artie	Daffyd	Lynn
Bardan	Dai	Maddox
Bevan	Davin	Meredith
Boden	Dillan	Merlin
Bowden	Dillon	Newlin
Bowen	Dylan	Owen
Bowie	Emrys	Reece
Bradan	Evan	Rhett
Bram	Gareth	Rhys
Bran	Gary	Romney
Brennan	Gavin	Taliesin
Brent	Gawain	Tristan
Bret	Gethin	Tristram
Bryce	Glyn	Trystan
Bryn	Gowan	Vaughn
Cadan	Ioan	Yale
Cadwur	Kay	

GIRLS

Arianwyn	Bryn	Ceri
Arwyn	Cal	Ceridwen
Blodeyn	Caron	Cerys
Blodwedd	Carwyn	Ciara
Brangwen	Cary	Crystin
Bronagh	Carys	Delwyn
Bronwen	Celyn	Dilwen

Dilys	Gweniver	Nerys
Eira	Gwyn	Olwen
Enid	Gwynedd	Orin
Ffion	Gwyneth	Rhianna
Fiona	Jennifer	Rhiannon
Gladys	Jenny	Rhonwen
Glenda	Kay	Rosslyn
Glenys	Kiera	Sabrina
Glynis	Llewella	Taffy
Guinevere	Lowri	Tegen
Gwen	Lynette	Ula
Gwendolin	Meredith	Valma
Gweneth	Morwenna	

6. Scottish names

BOYS

Alan
Alasdair
Alistair
Anghus
Archie
Boyd
Brian
Bryan
Cal
Callum
Cam
Cameron
Campbell
Clyde
Coleman
Conall
Craig
Dalziel
Darragh
Domhnall
Donal

Donald
Dougal
Douglas
Duncan
Dunmor
Euan
Ewan
Fife
Findlay
Finlay
Gillespie
Gilroy
Glen
Graeme
Grant
Hamish
Harvey
Iain
Ian
Jackie
Jock

Kyle
Leith
Lennox
Lesley
Lyle
Mac
Malcolm
McCartney
Morgan
Mungo
Murdoch
Murray
Neil
Quigley
Quinlan
Reid
Ronald
Rooney
Ross
Skelly

GIRLS

Aileen
Ailsa
Arlene
Elspeth
Glen

Isa
Isla
Janet
Kathleen
Kirstin

Kirsty
Lesley
Netta
Paisley

7. Cornish names

BOYS

Arthur
Artie
Benesek
Cador
Caradoc
Denzel

Gwithyen
Jacca
Jago
Jowan
Kevern
Lewyth

Mawgan
Piran
Rewan
Tristan
Trystan
Uther

GIRLS

Bennath
Blejan
Borra
Bronnen
Bryluen
Dellen
Demelza
Ebrel
Enor

Guinevere
Gwaynten
Gwiryon
Gwynder
Jenna
Kerensa
Kerra
Lamorna
Lowenna

Morenwyn
Morwenna
Rosenwyn
Senara
Talwyn
Wenna
Ysella

8. German names

BOYS

Abelard	Fulbright	Napolean
Adelbert	Godfrey	Norbert
Adolf	Gunther	Otto
Amory	Hansel	Robert
Anselm	Heinrich	Roger
Archibald	Heinz	Roland
Arnold	Helmut	Rolf
Bernhard	Herbert	Rory
Berthold	Hermann	Rudi
Bruno	Howe	Rudolf
Carl	Hubert	Rupert
Christhard	Hugo	Siegfried
Claus	Humbert	Siegmund
Colbert	Humphrey	Stefan
Conrad	Ingelbert	Ulrich
Dieter	Karl	Volker
Ebbo	Karsten	Waldo
Ernst	Keane	Wendel
Evert	Konrad	Wilhelm
Franz	Kurt	Willard
Frederik	Ludwig	Wolf
Friedrich	Luther	Wolfgang
Fritz	Lyulf	

GIRLS

Ada	Ebba	Emmeline
Adelheide	Edda	Ermentrude
Aleida	Elke	Frieda
Berta	Elsa	Gertrude
Bertha	Emil	Hedwig
Christa	Emily	Heidi
Dietlind	Emma	Hilda

Ilse
Katharina
Liese
Lorelei
Lotte
Luise
Lulu
Magda
Magdalene

Marlene
Mina
Mitzi
Romy
Rudy
Sieglind
Silke
Stefanie
Tilly

Trudy
Uda
Uta
Wendelin
Wilhelmina
Wilma
Winola
Wylda

9. Scandinavian names

BOYS

Ake
Amund
Anders
Ari
Arvid
Asmund
Axel
Bjorn
Broder
Caspar
Erik
Erland
Finn
Frode
Gunne
Gustav
Halvard
Harald
Havard
Ivar
Johanne
Kaspar
Kelsey
Knut
Kristian
Morten
Niels
Niklaus
Nordin
Ola
Olaf
Oman
Pal
Pitney
Quimby
Ragnar
Roald
Rothwell
Rune
Skip
Sondre
Soren
Sven
Sverre
Tor
Ulrik

GIRLS

Annika	Hulda	Rakel
Asa	Ikea	Rona
Asta	Ingrid	Runa
Astrid	Jensine	Saga
Barbro	Kaisa	Saskia
Birgit	Karita	Sassa
Bo	Katarina	Sigrid
Britt	Katharina	Silje
Christer	Kirsten	Siri
Dagmar	Kristen	Sissel
Dagna	Liv	Siv
Disa	Lovisa	Thora
Erika	Marna	Tilda
Freja	Merete	Tora
Gerd	Mia	Tordis
Gudrun	Nanna	Tyra
Helga	Ola	Ulrika
Hertha	Quinby	

10. Sanskrit names

BOYS

Ambar	Jyotis	Ramesh
Amrit	Kama	Ranjit
Anand	Karan	Ravi
Anil	Kiran	Sanjay
Arjun	Krishna	Sankara
Arun	Kumar	Shankar
Ashok	Lai	Sharma
Bharat	Lakshman	Sher
Bhima	Ljluka	Shiva
Chandan	Mahatma	Siddartha
Chandra	Mahendra	Suman
Deepak	Mahesh	Suresh
Dev	Mani	Surya
Devdan	Mohan	Taj
Dinesh	Mohinder	Tarun
Ganesh	Nanda	Ushnisha
Gautama	Narayan	Vamana
Ghandi	Narendra	Varuna
Gopal	Prakash	Vasudeva
Govinda	Prasad	Vidya
Hari	Prem	Vijay
Indra	Raj	Vimal
Jagdish	Rajendra	Vishnu
Jitender	Rajiv	Wassily

GIRLS

Ambar	Avara	Dharma
Amrita	Bala	Durga
Ananda	Chandani	Gita
Anila	Chandi	Indira
Aruna	Chandra	Jalini
Asha	Devika	Jama

Jarita	Mohana	Shakti
Jaya	Nagini	Shakuntala
Jyoti	Nalini	Shamra
Kali	Opal	Shanti
Kalinda	Padma	Sharmila
Kalpana	Parminder	Sheela
Kalyani	Parvati	Sher
Kama	Prema	Shobhana
Kamala	Priya	Sita
Kanti	Purnima	Sitara
Kumari	Radha	Sujata
Lakshmi	Rajani	Sunita
Lalita	Rani	Topaz
Leela	Rati	Uma
Madhuri	Rohana	Usha
Malati	Rukmini	Vasanti
Mani	Sanila	Veda
Manjusha	Sarisha	Vidya
Meena	Saroja	Vimala

11. Arabic names

BOYS

Abbas	Faysal	Khalid
Abdel	Feroz	Khalif
Abdullah	Ferran	Khalil
Abir	Firdos	Latif
Adil	Gamal	Mahmood
Adnan	Ghassan	Mahomet
Ahmed	Ginton	Majid
Akbar	Habib	Malik
Akeem	Hadi	Mansoor
Akil	Hafiz	Masud
Akram	Hakim	Mohammed
Aladdin	Hamal	Mubarak
Ali	Hamid	Muhammad
Alim	Hani	Mukhtar
Amal	Hasim	Nabil
Amin	Hassan	Nadir
Amir	Hussain	Nasir
Ansari	Imam	Nassir
Anwar	Jabir	Nuri
Ashraf	Jaleel	Omar
Asim	Jalil	Osman
Aswad	Jamal	Qabil
Azim	Kadin	Qadir
Aziz	Kadir	Qasim
Bashir	Kalid	Quasim
Basim	Kalil	Rafi
Bilal	Kamal	Rafiq
Cemal	Kamil	Rahman
Emir	Karim	Rashid
Fadil	Kasim	Rauf
Faisal	Kateb	Sabir
Farid	Kedar	Sadik
Farook	Kemal	Salah

Salim
Salman
Sarni
Sayed
Seif
Selim
Seyed
Shafiq
Shakar
Shakir

Sharif
Shunnar
Tahir
Tamir
Tariq
Umar
Usman
Wahib
Walid
Wasim

Xerxes
Yasir
Yazid
Zade
Zafar
Zahir
Zaki
Zia

GIRLS

Aaliyah
Abia
Abir
Adar
Adara
Adiba
Adila
Adiva
Afraima
Aiesha
Ain
Aisha
Akila
Akilah
Ali
Alima
Aliya
Aliyah
Almira
Alzena
Amala
Amani
Amber
Ambra
Ameerah

Amina
Amira
Anan
Anisa
Annissa
Atifa
Atiya
Aziza
Azra
Barakah
Basimah
Bibi
Cala
Cantara
Elma
Esther
Fadila
Faiza
Farah
Farida
Fatima
Fatin
Ghada
Habiba
Hadya

Haifa
Hana
Hasna
Hayfa
Helima
Imam
Iman
Isra
Israt
Jala
Jalila
Jamal
Jamelia
Jamila
Jamilah
Janan
Janna
Jarnila
Jasmine
Jehan
Jira
Kadira
Kaela
Kalila
Kamil

Kamilah	Noor	Shakira
Karida	Noya	Sultana
Karima	Oma	Sumehra
Kebira	Qadira	Tahira
Khalida	Qamra	Tahirah
Latifa	Rabi	Thana
Leila	Raja	Thara
Lila	Rana	Tulin
Lilith	Rashida	Ulima
Lina	Roxanna	Umar
Lyla	Roxanne	Vega
Mahala	Roxy	Wahiba
Malak	Sabah	Wahida
Malika	Sabira	Walida
Matana	Saffron	Wasima
Maysa	Safia	Widjan
Medina	Sahar	Yasmina
Melek	Sahara	Yusra
Muna	Saida	Zada
Munira	Sakinah	Zadie
Muriel	Salima	Zahara
Myiesha	Salimah	Zahra
Nabila	Salwa	Zaina
Nada	Samirah	Zakira
Nadira	Samma	Zarifa
Nafeeza	Sana	Zenith
Nawal	Saree	Zia
Nazirah	Sawsan	Zohra
Nimah	Shahira	Zulema

12. French names

BOYS

Aimé
Alain
Alec
Aleron
Alexandre
Amaury
Ancel
André
Antoine
Anton
Armand
Armani
Arnaud
Auguste
Augustin
Bailey
Beau
Beaumont
Benoît
Bertrand
Camilo
Charles
Charlie
Chase
Chevalier
Christophe
Darell
Darryl
Dartagnan
Didier
Diggory
Dominique

Donatien
Édouard
Émile
Esme
Étienne
Farquar
Fran
François
Fraser
Frasier
Frédéric
Gérard
Germain
Gervaise
Grégoire
Henri
Honoré
Jacques
Jean
Jermaine
Julian
Laurent
Leroy
Louis
Luc
Lucas
Macy
Marcel
Marmion
Matthieu
Melville
Merrill

Michel
Moore
Morell
Nicolas
Noe
Noël
Norville
Olivier
Percival
Percy
Philippe
Pierre
Ray
Raymond
Rémy
René
Roy
Saville
Serge
Seymore
Sidney
Sorrel
Stéphane
Talbot
Théodore
Théophile
Thierry
Vivian
Xavier
Yves
Zacharie

GIRLS

Adèle
Adrienne
Aerien
Agathe
Aimée
Alea
Alize
Amalie
Amarante
Amélie
Amerique
Anaïs
Anastasie
Andrée
Ange
Anjanette
Anouk
Antoinette
Astrid
Aurélie
Aurore
Avril
Babette
Bailey
Bella
Belle
Bernadette
Bijou
Bonte
Brie
Brier
Brigitte
Capucine
Caresse
Caron
Cécile

Chanel
Chanelle
Chantal
Chante
Charlene
Charlize
Charlotte
Chaton
Cheryl
Christelle
Christiane
Christine
Claudette
Claudine
Clémence
Colette
Corinne
Courtney
Danielle
Darlene
Deja
Delice
Desiree
Diamanta
Diane
Dior
Dominique
Dore
Doreen
Dori
Dorothée
Élise
Elle
Elodie
Élodie
Eloise

Émilie
Emmanuelle
Fleurette
Fossetta
Françoise
Frédérique
Gabrielle
Garland
Gay
Geneva
Geneviève
Germaine
Harriette
Hélène
Henriette
Hortense
Inès
Isabelle
Jacqueline
Jacquetta
Jamais
Janelle
Jean
Jeanne
Jeannine
Jolie
Josette
Juillet
Juliette
Jumelle
Laure
Leala
Linette
Lorraine
Louise
Mabel

Mai	Nathalie	Satine
Malory	Nettie	Shance
Manon	Nicole	Sheryl
Marcelle	Noelle	Sigourney
Mardi	Océane	Soleil
Margaux	Odette	Sophie
Margot	Olivie	Susanne
Marianne	Orene	Sylvie
Marie	Page	Tempest
Marine	Pascale	Thérèse
Marjorie	Paulette	Valérie
Marvelle	Pauline	Véronique
Maryse	Philippine	Victoire
Mathilde	Raissa	Villette
Merise	Renée	Virginie
Michèle	Roche	Vivienne
Mignon	Rochelle	Voletta
Monique	Royale	Yvonne
Musique	Safran	
Nanette	Saison	

13. Italian names

BOYS

Abbondanzio
Adalfredo
Adalgisio
Adalrico
Adriano
Alarico
Alberico
Alberto
Aldo
Alessio
Alfonsino
Alfredo
Alvaro
Amalio
Amaranto
Amerigo
Angelo
Antonio
Ariosto
Armando
Basso
Benito
Bernardo
Bertoldo
Biagio
Bonifacio
Boris
Bruno
Caio
Camillo
Carisio
Carlo
Cassio

Cataldo
Celio
Cesare
Cherubino
Cino
Cipriano
Claudio
Concordio
Cornelio
Cosimo
Costanzo
Cristiano
Dante
Dario
Demetrio
Diego
Dimitri
Dino
Domenico
Durante
Eberardo
Edilio
Edmondo
Eduardo
Elia
Eliano
Eligio
Emanuele
Emidio
Emilio
Ennio
Enrico
Ercole

Eric
Erizo
Eros
Ezio
Fabio
Fabrizio
Fausto
Federico
Ferdinando
Ferruccio
Fidenzio
Filiberto
Filippo
Fiorello
Fiorenzo
Firenze
Flavio
Fosco
Francesco
Franco
Furio
Gabriele
Galileo
Gandolfo
Gaspare
Gennaro
Geraldo
Geronimo
Giancarlo
Gianetto
Gianfranco
Gianni
Gildo

Gino	Nereo	Roland
Giorgio	Nino	Rolando
Giovanni	Olindo	Romano
Giuseppe	Olivero	Romeo
Gregorio	Omero	Romolo
Guido	Oreste	Rufino
Lamberto	Orlando	Salvatore
Landro	Oronzo	Salvo
Leo	Orso	Samuele
Leonardo	Ortensio	Sante
Leone	Oscar	Santo
Leopoldo	Ottone	Saverio
Liberio	Ovidio	Serafino
Libero	Paciano	Sergio
Lisandro	Palmiro	Severo
Lorenzo	Paolo	Silvano
Luca	Piero	Silvestro
Luciano	Pietro	Silvio
Lucio	Pio	Siro
Lucius	Placido	Stefano
Luigi	Prospero	Terenzio
Manuel	Raimondo	Tito
Marcello	Ramiro	Tommaso
Marco	Raul	Umberto
Mariano	Renato	Uriele
Mario	Ricardo	Valentino
Martino	Rinaldo	Valerio
Massimo	Roberto	Vincenzo
Michelangelo	Rocco	Vitale
Muzio	Rodolfo	Vito
Narciso	Rodrigo	Vittore

GIRLS

Abela	Adalgisa	Adelinda
Abelina	Adelaide	Adriana
Ada	Adelfina	Alberta
Adalberta	Adelia	Albertina

Albina	Carla	Elena
Alda	Carmela	Eleonora
Alfonsina	Carola	Eliana
Alfreda	Carolina	Elisa
Alfredina	Cassandra	Elisabetta
Alida	Catena	Ella
Alma	Caterina	Elsa
Aloisia	Cecilia	Elvia
Alvisa	Celeste	Elvira
Amalia	Cesarina	Emanuela
Ambretta	Chiara	Emilia
Angelica	Ciara	Emma
Angelina	Cinzia	Enrica
Anita	Cirilla	Eriza
Anna	Clara	Ermenegilda
Anna Maria	Claudia	Ernesta
Annabella	Cora	Eva
Annabel	Corinna	Fabiana
Antonella	Cornelia	Fabiola
Antonietta	Crispina	Fabrizia
Arabella	Cristiano	Fausta
Arianna	Cristina	Federica
Artemisia	Dalia	Fedra
Aurelia	Dalila	Felicita
Aurora	Damiana	Ferdinanda
Barbara	Daniela	Filiberta
Batilda	Daphne	Filippa
Beatrice	Daria	Fiore
Belinda	Deborah	Fiorenze
Berenice	Delfina	Fioretta
Berta	Delinda	Flavia
Bianca	Delmina	Fosca
Bibiana	Demetria	Franca
Brigida	Dina	Francesca
Bruna	Domenica	Francine
Camelia	Donatella	Frida
Camilla	Dorotea	Gabriella
Candida	Elda	Gemma

Geraldina	Lia	Miriam
Giada	Libera	Morgana
Gianna	Licia	Nadia
Gilda	Lidia	Natalia
Gina	Liliana	Natascia
Ginevra	Lina	Neera
Giorgia	Linda	Nella
Giovanna	Livia	Nicoletta
Giselda	Lorena	Nora
Gisella	Lorenza	Norma
Giselle	Lorna	Novella
Gloria	Luana	Odetta
Grazia	Lucia	Olga
Graziella	Luciana	Ortensia
Greta	Lucilla	Palmira
Guendalina	Lucrezia	Paola
Ida	Luigia	Penelope
Ileana	Luisa	Petronilla
Imelda	Luisella	Pia
Ines	Maddalena	Priscilla
Irene	Maia	Regina
Irma	Manuela	Renata
Irmina	Mara	Rina
Isa	Marcella	Rita
Isabella	Mareta	Roberta
Isidora	Maria	Robina
Isotta	Marianna	Romilda
Iva	Marina	Romola
Ivana	Marisa	Rosalia
Lara	Marta	Rosanna
Lavinia	Martina	Rosaria
Lea	Marzia	Rosetta
Leda	Matilde	Rosina
Leila	Melissa	Rosita
Lelia	Michela	Rossana
Leonida	Michelina	Rufina
Letizia	Miranda	Sabina
Letteria	Mirella	Sabrina

Sandra	Stefania	Veronica
Santa	Susanna	Viola
Santina	Tamara	Violanda
Sara	Teresa	Violetta
Selena	Tiziana	Virginia
Serena	Tullia	Vittoria
Silvana	Vala	Viviana
Silvia	Valentina	Wanda
Simona	Vanna	
Sofia	Vera	

14. Spanish names

BOYS

Abejundio	Esteban	Nevada
Agustin	Fausto	Orlando
Alarico	Federico	Othello
Alejandro	Felipe	Oziel
Alfonso	Ferdinando	Pablo
Alonso	Fernando	Pacifico
Alvaro	Francisco	Pancho
Amador	Galeno	Paolo
Amato	Gambero	Pedro
Amistad	Garcia	Pepe
Antonio	Gentil	Rafael
Armando	Gomez	Ramiro
Carlos	Guillermo	Ramon
Castel	Hernando	Renaldo
Caton	Iago	Rico
Celio	Isidro	Roderigo
Chale	Jaguar	Rodolfo
Cid	Javier	Rodrigo
Claudio	Jeremias	Rogelio
Cornelio	Jorge	Salado
Cortes	Jose	Salvador
Cristo	Juan	Sancho
Cruze	Leonardo	Santiago
Darien	Lucio	Santos
Demetrius	Luis	Senon
Desidirio	Manuel	Seville
Devante	Marco	Tajo
Diego	Miguel	Tomas
Efrain	Natal	Vittorio
Emilio	Navarro	Xavier
Enrique	Neron	Zavier

GIRLS

Adoncia	Fidelia	Neva
Alatea	Francisca	Nevada
Aldonza	Galaxia	Numa
Alejandra	Gitana	Olalla
Alita	Hermosa	Olino
Allegra	Imelda	Pacifica
Amata	Isabel	Paloma
Belicia	Isleta	Patia
Belita	Jaimica	Pepa
Bonita	Jaira	Pepita
Buena	Juana	Perla
Carmelita	Juanita	Pilar
Carmen	Karlotta	Ria
Catalina	Kesare	Rica
Chiquita	Latoya	Rosario
Cochiti	Liani	Rosita
Coco	Lona	Salvadora
Consuelo	Lourdes	Sandia
Corazon	Lucetta	Savanna
Cortesia	Lucia	Sevilla
Delma	Luigia	Socorro
Delores	Lujuana	Solana
Dolores	Lynda	Tia
Dominga	Madra	Tierra
Dorota	Manuela	Tulia
Drina	Maribel	Ventura
Duena	Mariposa	Vina
Eldora	Mariquita	Vittoria
Elvira	Marita	Xaviera
Engracia	Marta	Xiomara
Enrica	Melisenda	Xuxa
Esmeralda	Melosa	Xylia
Esperanza	Mercedes	Yomaris
Ester	Mireya	Ysobel
Felipa	Mora	Zafiro

15. Russian names

BOYS

Afanasi	Gennadi	Sasha
Akim	Grigor	Sergei
Alek	Igor	Vadim
Aleksander	Ilya	Vanya
Aleksei	Ivan	Vasili
Alexei	Karl	Vassilly
Andrei	Kazimir	Vassily
Anisim	Kolya	Viktor
Bogdan	Luka	Vitali
Boris	Lyov	Vitya
Danil	Mikhail	Vlad
Dima	Mikula	Vladisav
Dimitri	Misha	Vladja
Dmitri	Nikita	Vladmir
Faddei	Nikolai	Volodya
Fedot	Oleg	Volya
Feofilakt	Pasha	Yakim
Feofilart	Pavel	Yakov
Ferapont	Petya	Yaroslav
Foma	Radko	Yasha
Garsah	Radosalve	Yuri
Gavril	Rurik	Zakhar

GIRLS

Agafaya	Anastasia	Fedora
Aglaya	Anouska	Gala
Agnessa	Antonina	Galina
Akilina	Anushka	Galya
Aksinya	Arina	Irina
Aleksandra	Asya	Ivana
Aleksandrina	Ayn	Jana
Alyona	Bogdana	Katinka

Katya
Kenya
Lana
Larisa
Larissa
Lizaveta
Ludmila
Lyuba
Mariya
Mikhaila
Milena
Misha
Nadine
Nadya

Nastasia
Natasha
Polina
Raina
Raya
Roksana
Rula
Sacha
Sasha
Sofiya
Sonya
Stasya
Sveta
Svetlana

Tanya
Tasha
Valeska
Vanna
Vladisalva
Vladmira
Vonda
Yaromira
Yelena
Zhenya
Zina
Zinaida
Zinovia

16. American names

BOYS

Audey	Darrick	Kale
Barlow	Davon	Kyzer
Booker	Dewey	Lynshawn
Boone	Dirk	Maverick
Bradley	Duke	Money
Brando	Durand	Newbie
Brant	Dwight	Ox
Bubba	Eli	Perry
Buck	Emmett	Sparky
Butch	Everley	Texas
Calhoun	Fargo	Tipple
Carson	Hobart	Trey
Chance	Houston	Tyonne
Chaz	Jaycee	Van
Chuck	Jazz	Xen
Clay	Jefferson	Xyle
Clayton	Jerral	Yadon
Cobain	Jonte	Yancy
Dadrian	Jorell	Zaie
Dakota	Kacy	Zain

GIRLS

Annisa	Coretta	Hawlee
Arlene	Dakota	Izzy
Arlinda	Deandra	Jacey
Babe	Dewi	Jadelyn
Beyonce	Dolly	Jaxine
Candice	Dusty	Jay
Cayla	Elegy	Jeri
Cody	Ember	Jessalyn
Cookie	Etenia	Jocelyn
Cora	Geena	Joplin

Kady	McKayla	Sherilyn
Kalisa	Nebraska	Shine
Kenna	Olaide	Taffeta
Kiana	Peppy	Tibby
Kodi	Rabbit	Toffey
Krystal	Richelle	True
Leona	Ricky	Truly
Lucky	Sea	Velma
Macey	Shania	Winona
Marlene	Shawnee	Yancey

17. Australian names

BOYS

Adoni	Derain	Marron
Akama	Dheran	Matari
Allambee	Dorak	Monti
Amaroo	Ganan	Mowan
Araluen	Gelar	Nambur
Balun	Jarrah	Nardu
Banjora	Jerara	Narrah
Bardo	Jirra	Nioka
Barega	Kari	Orad
Barwon	Kolet	Pindan
Cobar	Koorong	Uwan
Coorain	Kulan	Warra
Daku	Lowan	Yarran
Darel	Maka	

GIRLS

Akala	Darri	Kylie
Alinga	Ekala	Orana
Alkina	Ellin	Pangari
Alkira	Gedala	Pierah
Amarina	Ghera	Tallara
Apanie	Gulara	Tarana
Araluen	Hanya	Tathra
Arika	Jannali	Tirranna
Arinya	Jarrah	Ulla
Bakana	Jiba	Umina
Barina	Jirra	Yani
Bega	Kadee	Yara
Binda	Kaiya	Yindi
Camira	Kala	
Coorah	Kiah	

18. African names

BOYS

Abdalla
Abdul
Abedi
Abiola
Afam
Baakir
Babu
Badrani
Bello
Chacha
Chibale
Chimalsi
Daktari
Diallo
Elewa
Eze
Fahim
Farhani

Ghalib
Haamid
Iman
Jaafar
Kofi
Kosey
Maalik
Mandela
Moswen
Muhammed
Naasir
Nanji
Nassor
Odongo
Paki
Rafiki
Rashad
Rasul

Saad
Saeed
Said
Salaam
Senwe
Tahir
Taji
Talib
Ubora
Ulan
Umar
Waitimu
Yohance
Zahir
Zareb
Zuri

GIRLS

Aba
Abayomi
Abebi
Abeo
Abla
Adaeze
Adande
Adanma
Adanna
Adanne
Adero
Adjua

Adwin
Adzo
Afam
Afi
Agbeko
Aidoo
Akili
Akuabia
Akuako
Akwate
Alaba
Alaezi

Alyetoro
Ama
Asha
Ayanna
Baako
Baba
Badu
Bahati
Benada
Binah
Binta
Bisa

Bunme	Keisha	Sisi
Chiku	Kia	Siti
Chinue	Layla	Tabita
Damisi	Lisha	Talibah
Doli	Maisha	Tamika
Efia	Malika	Tawia
Eshe	Omesha	Tisha
Fadhila	Oni	Uzima
Ghalyela	Paka	Uzuri
Gimbya	Pulika	Wangari
Haiba	Quisha	Winna
Halla	Rafiya	Yaa
Hamida	Raisa	Yakini
Hanna	Ridhaa	Zalika
Imena	Saada	Zawadi
Jalia	Sabra	Zuwina
Kamaria	Safari	
Kamili	Shukuma	

19. Names derived from literature

BOYS

Aragorn	*The Lord of the Rings* by J. R. R. Tolkien
Aramis	*The Three Musketeers* by Alexandre Dumas
Caspian	*Prince Caspian* by C. S. Lewis
Cassio	*Othello* by William Shakespeare
Darcy	*Pride and Prejudice* by Jane Austen
Dorian	*The Picture of Dorian Gray* by Oscar Wilde
Hamlet	*Hamlet* by William Shakespeare
Iago	Othello by William Shakespeare
Jem	*To Kill a Mockingbird* by Harper Lee, *Jamaica Inn* by Daphne du Maurier
Lestat	*Vampire Chronicles* by Anne Rice
Oberon	*A Midsummer Night's Dream* by William Shakespeare
Sawyer	*The Adventures of Tom Sawyer* by Mark Twain
Sherlock	*The Adventures of SherlockHolmes* by Sir Arthur Conan Doyle
Sinbad	*The Book of 1001 Arabian Nights*
Yorick	*Hamlet* by William Shakespeare

GIRLS

Arwen	*The Lord of the Rings* by J. R. R. Tolkien
Belphoebe	*The Faeirie Queen* by Edmund Spenser
Calypso	*Odyssey* by Homer
Dulcinea	*Don Quixote* by Miguel de Cervantes
Eowyn	*The Lord of the Rings* by J. R. R. Tolkien
Eponin	*Les Misérables* by Victor Hugo
Galadriel	*The Lord of the Rings* by J. R. R. Tolkien
Gyneth	*The Bridal of Triermain* by Sir Walter Scott
Idril	*The Silmarillion* by J. R. R. Tolkien
Jessica	*The Merchant of Venice* by Shakespeare
Miranda	*The Tempest* by William Shakespeare
Orinthia	*The Apple Cart* by George Bernard Shaw
Wendy	*Peter Pan* by J. M. Barrie

20. Names inspired by nature

BOYS

Acorn	Forest	Rowan
Ash	Hail	Smokey
Breeze	Heath	Storm
Cliff	Hurricane	Tor
Cyclone	Ice	Vernon
Fire	Rocky	Woody

GIRLS

Apple	Eartha	Raindrop
Autumn	Fen	Ripple
Berry	Fern	Shamrock
Blossom	Flower	Sky
Bramble	Gaia	Snow
Brooke	Leaf	Snowflake
Cirrus	Luna	Spring
Cloud	Moon	Summer
Crystal	Ocean	Sunset
Dandelion	Pebbles	Sunshine
Dawn	Petal	
Dusk	Rain	

21. Names from mythology

BOYS

Achilles	Hercules	Sirius
Adonis	Jason	Thor
Ambrose	Mark	Zeus
Apollo	Martin	
Damian	Paris	

GIRLS

Aurora	Helen	Narcissa
Calypso	Hera	Penelope
Cassandra	Iris	Phoebe
Cynthia	Leda	Sybil
Daphne	Martina	Venus
Denise	Minerva	

22. Spiritual names

BOYS

Angelo	Idol	Spirit
Avalon	Nirvana	Star
Free	Pax	Truth
Hevan	Soul	Utope

GIRLS

Angel	Dream	Paradise
Bliss	Elysia	Serendipity
Deity	Harmony	Sky
Destiny	Heaven	
Divine	Infinity	

23. Timeless names

BOYS

Alexander	John	Robert
Andrew	Mark	Simon
Daniel	Matthew	Thomas
David	Michael	William
Edward	Nicholas	
James	Peter	

GIRLS

Alison	Emma	Maria
Anne	Jane	Rachel
Catherine	Joanna	Rebecca
Claire	Julia	Sarah
Elizabeth	Laura	Victoria

24. Names that will date

BOYS

Brooklyn	Joshua	Preston
Cade	Leonardo	Shayne
Cruz	Mackenzie	Tyler
Heath	Noah	Unique
Jayden	Orlando	Zane

GIRLS

Britney	Jordan	Ruby
Chanelle	Molly	Scarlett
Halle	Paris	Unique
Keira	Peaches	
Kylie	Poppy	

25. Playground-proof names

BOYS

Adam	Jack	Michael
Andrew	James	Stephen
Ben	John	Thomas
Carl	Lee	
David	Mark	

GIRLS

Amy	Jenny	Sarah
Catherine	Kate	Sophie
Charlotte	Lucy	Zoe
Chloe	Rachel	
Emma	Rebecca	

Notes

Notes